AURA GARDEN GUIDES

Ulrike Leyhe

Grasses and Ferns

AURA BOOKS

Aura Garden Guides

Grasses and Ferns

Ulrike Leyhe

Original German-language edition:
Gräser und Farne: Die schönsten Arten und Sorten – Auswählen, Gestalten, Pflegen
© 2003 BLV Verlagsgesellschaft mbH, Munich, Germany

This edition produced by:
Transedition Limited for
Aura Books, Bicester, and first published in 2005

English-language edition:
© 2005 Advanced Marketing (UK) Ltd, Bicester, England

English-language translation by:
Andrew Shackleton for Translate-a-Book,
a division of Transedition Ltd, Oxford

Typesetting by:
Asgard Publishing Services, Leeds

10 9 8 7 6 5 4 3
Printed in Dubai

ISBN 1 903938 74 0

Photo credits:
Adams: 46, 50, 96; Borstell: 2/3, 14, 15, 17b, 18 19t, 24, 27b, 30b, 31b, 32t, b, 34, 41t, 45t, b, 48 53, 55, 57, 58t, 60, 63, 65tl, bl, br, 67tr, 71t, 73. 75, 76, 78, 89, 90, 92, 93; Brand: 70t, b; GBA/Didillon: 6, 37, 39b, 42; GBA/GPL: 68t; Hagen: 9t, b, 20, 21b, 22, 31t, 33, 47, 52t, b, 67tm, 84t, 85, 86, 87; Leyhe: 11, 25t, 40, 64, 77b, 81, 82b, 83l, 91; Pforr: 8, 23, 66, 67bl; Redeleit: 84b; Reinhard: 7, 10t, 29t, b, 36b, 43, 54, 56t, 59, 62, 65tr, 67br, 71b, 72, 74, 79, 88; Seidl: 4, 10t/inset, 16t, 17t, 21t, 25b, 26, 27t, 28 35, 36t, 39t, 41b, 44, 49, 51, 55t, 56b, 58b, 61t, 61b, 67tl, 69; Stannat: 38; Strauss: 10b, 12, 16b 19b, 30t, 68b, 80, 82t, 83r.

Contents

Inconspicuous yet indispensable

Grasses and ferns were among the first plants to be introduced into gardens as green companion plants. But it was a long time before they finally emerged from the shadows and came to be recognised as plants in their own right. Nowadays, however, grasses and ferns have become an indispensable element of garden design.

Many true grasses produce attractive flowers in the form of spikes, panicles or racemes.

Green companion plants

Grasses and ferns are often lumped together by gardeners, although they are completely unrelated to each other from a botanical point of view.

However, they have one important factor in common, in that their leaves are normally the main visual feature. But whereas grasses may have decorative flowers too, ferns are prized purely for their green fronds.

A little botany

From a horticultural point of view, ferns (some of which are evergreen) and most grasses belong to the category of herbaceous perennials. Bamboos are

◄ Ferns – and some grasses too – make excellent foliage plants for shady places. The more varied the combination of leaf patterns, the more interesting the display.

an exception to this – they are grasses with woody stems, which makes them more like shrubs. There are also many annual grasses that are of great decorative value.

Grasses

The term 'grass' is used to describe members of three families of plants: the Poaceae, or true grasses, the Cyperaceae, comprising sedges and reeds, and the Juncaceae, or rushes. These are three of the largest families of plants, with around 13,000 species altogether. Botanically speaking, only the Poaceae are grasses as such. But all three families share similar characteristics, both visually and in terms of their use, so most gardeners treat all of them as grasses.

The **true grasses** are by far the most important of the three families, with as many as 9,000 species spread all over the globe, often covering large

areas such as prairies and savannahs.

Apart from the various ornamental grasses, this family contains a large number of crop species, including grasses for grazing and many different grains, not to mention maize, sugar cane, rice and some tropical bamboos.

The main distinguishing features of the true grasses are their round, hollow stems, which are divided by nodes. The leaves grow from the nodes or from the base of the stems. The flowers usually grow in loose panicles or narrow spikes from the top of a stem.

The flowers of sedges and reeds (this plant is a sedge) are visually less striking than those of true grasses, which often have considerable decorative value.

Sedges and reeds are distinguished from true grasses by their nodeless stems with a triangular cross-section. The stems of **rushes** are round. In both cases the stems are not hollow but filled with pith.

Grass flowers

Grasses produce large numbers of small, insignificant flowers. As grasses are pollinated by the wind, they have no need of brightly coloured petals to attract insects.

The tiny flowers are borne in spikelets that in turn are grouped in inflorescences. Depending on their shape, the inflorescences are known as spikes (ears), racemes or panicles, and in many grasses they are of great ornamental value.

The tiny scales (glumes) that form over the spikelets often have smooth or feathery bristles (awns) that add to the charm of grasses such as *Stipa* (feather grass) or *Hordeum jubatum* (foxtail barley).

Grasses in their natural surroundings

The natural habitats of grasses range widely from sea coastlines to high mountains, and these plants are at home in every continent of the world. In many regions they constitute the most significant element of the vegetation, such as across the vast prairies and savannahs of North and South America, or on the steppes of Central Asia. Grasses are in fact present throughout the natural world. This means that there are suitable grasses for every part of a garden.

Bamboos

Bamboos have a special place among the grasses. There are some 1,500 species in all, which make up a subfamily of the Poaceae or true grasses.

Bamboos are significantly different from other grasses in having woody perennial stems. However, they are not true shrubs, because their stems, despite being woody, are not subject to secondary growth – i.e. they don't become thicker with age – and only last for some ten years at the very most.

Outer appearance

A bamboo plant is made up of an underground **rhizome**, a **stem** or **cane** and **leaf-bearing twigs**.

Bamboo canes
The stem or cane is the most decorative part of a bamboo plant. Depending on the species, stems may vary in length from 20 cm (8 in) to 40 m (130 ft). In temperate latitudes they rarely grow taller than 6–8 m (20–26 ft). Most bamboo species have green stems, but there are some with yellow, brown, black or even reddish-coloured ones. Bamboo

canes may also have speckles or stripes in one or more colours.

Bamboo canes grow very fast, each reaching its full height within a couple of months. They are not subject to any secondary growth or thickening, so their diameter remains unchanged from when they first appear. Only when a cane has reached its final height does it start to form twigs and leaves, and it will not grow any taller than in the year it first sprouts. However, healthy young plants will tend to produce thicker and taller canes during subsequent years. Bamboo canes

Bamboo canes are particularly attractive. Although normally green, they may also be yellow, black or brownish in colour.

will generally last for about five to seven years, after which they will turn pale, wither and eventually die.

Foliage

Bamboo leaves are evergreen but don't last very long. A few are shed every spring to be replaced by new ones. The old leaves should be left on the ground, as they rot down quickly to provide valuable nutrients for the plant's further development.

Bamboo rhizomes

Bamboo stems grow from underground rhizomes, which develop mainly in the early summer when the stems and twigs have finished growing. They spread and intertwine over the years to form a dense, branching network.

The rhizomes grow in two distinct ways, depending on the species of bamboo. Some species are **clump-forming** while others spread by means of **runners**, and it is the rhizomes that determine the kind of growth.

Clump-forming bamboos have short, compact rhizomes that grow upwards to form new stems. This process results in dense clumps of stems that

Bamboo rhizomes are hard and pointed. As bamboos have no secondary growth, the rhizomes give an immediate indication of how thick the stem will be.

gradually spread outwards. *Fargesia* is a well-known example of a clump-forming bamboo.

Bamboos that form runners have long, thin rhizomes that grow horizontally. New stems develop from buds in the rhizomes. The runners can spread a long way to cover a wide area, and often lie close to the surface of the soil.

Bamboo flowers

Unlike the herbaceous grasses, bamboos have rather uninteresting flowers.

From a horticultural point of view, bamboo flowers are not so much insignificant as undesirable, as they weaken the plant to the extent that it may even die. This is probably why bamboos normally flower so rarely, at intervals of 20–30 years, or even 80–120 years, depending on the species.

Perhaps the best-known example of this phenomenon was in the mid-1990s, when vast numbers of Muriel bamboos (*Fargesia murieliae*) came into flower all over the world, and died of exhaustion from the process of seeding.

This isn't true of all the bamboos. *Pleioblastus* species are scarcely affected by flowering, while *Phyllostachys* will recover again after pruning and plenty of feeding.

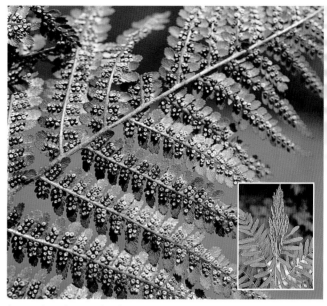

In many ferns the spore-bearing structures, or sporangia, can be found on the underside of the fronds. Some species such as the royal fern (see inset) develop separate spore-bearing fronds.

Bamboo flowers are generally undesirable, as in many cases they cause the plant to die of exhaustion.

Ferns

Ferns are among the oldest of plants, having originated some 400 million years ago. Most species later became extinct, but during the Carboniferous period (around 300 million years ago) the world was dominated by ferns and their relatives, the horsetails and club mosses. Aeons later, these plants were to provide energy in the form of coal.

From an evolutionary point of view, ferns form the transition between non-flowering and flowering plants. They are an entirely separate group of plants that develop spores instead of flowers and seeds.

There are far fewer species of ferns nowadays than during Carboniferous times, with some 220 genera and approximately 9,000 species. Most fern species are native to tropical regions, where some of them – the so-called **tree ferns** – grow to the size of trees. There are only about 50 species of ferns that are native to this country.

Ferns constitute a sharply defined and very unified group among the perennials. Our native wild ferns are all herbaceous plants, some of which are deciduous while others are evergreen.

The leaves, which are known as **fronds**, are surprisingly varied in form. Some species have simple fronds, while most have compound fronds divided into multiple arrays. They range in colour from light green to dark green, reddish or even silvery grey.

Spores instead of seeds

Ferns don't produce seeds but spores. The spore-bearing structures, or sporangia, form clusters, known as sori, which

Ferns are particularly attractive in the spring as the fronds unfurl, looking like tiny bishops' crooks.

may be round or linear in form and are mostly to be found on the underside of some of the fronds. Such fronds are described as fertile, while the others are sterile because they have no sporangia.

In most ferns the sterile and fertile fronds look much the same when viewed from above. But there are some ferns where the fertile fronds look very different from the sterile ones – a phenomenon known as heterophyllia. This is found in species such as the ostrich (or shuttlecock) fern (*Matteuccia struthiopteris*) and the royal fern (*Osmunda regalis*).

In the ostrich fern, the fertile fronds appear at the end of the growing season, after the sterile fronds, and are completely different in appearance. In the royal fern, the spore-bearing stalks appear as separate structures from the top section of the fronds (see photo inset opposite), and serve no purpose apart from spore production.

Spring growth in ferns

Ferns are particularly attractive in the spring as the fronds begin to sprout. They are in fact already formed in the autumn

ready for the next year. They are protected by tiny scale-like leaves and additionally by the old fronds and autumn leaf fall. Being so well prepared means that they can sprout very quickly in the spring. The sprouting fronds look especially attractive as they unfurl, each resembling a tiny bishop's crook.

at a glance

- Grasses and ferns fulfil an important role in gardens as green companion plants for perennials and shrubs.

- From a botanical point of view, ferns and grasses are two completely unrelated groups of plants.

- These plants have one important aspect in common, which is that their leaves and growth habits are their main ornamental features.

- Ferns form a distinct and unified group among the herbaceous perennials, and can only be used as ornamental foliage plants.

- Ornamental grasses can be divided into annual grasses, herbaceous perennial grasses and woody-stemmed bamboos.

The best grasses and ferns

Although grasses and ferns were late to arrive in gardens as plants in their own right, there is a vast range of them available nowadays from garden centres and plant nurseries. Below is a selection of the best grasses and ferns from among the large number of species and varieties on offer.

The plant profiles below describe the general shape of the plants, and their leaves and flowers, then give some advice on the best planting locations, treatment and uses of each plant. In many cases, particular varieties of a plant are recommended. The symbols provide a quick summary of the flowering season, growth height and light requirements.

Botanical names

Full botanical names are used throughout to avoid confusion. This is because common names vary greatly between different regions, which makes the use of botanical names essential.

The specific name of a plant – *Arundo donax*, for example – is often supplemented by a cultivar name that is placed in inverted commas – for instance, *Arundo donax* 'Macrophylla'.

Where two species are crossed with one another to produce a hybrid, this is indicated by a multiplication sign (×). There is an example of this in the genus *Calamagrostis*, where the variety 'Karl Foerster' derives from a naturally occurring hybrid between *Calamagrostis epigejos* and *Calamagrostis arundinacea* that is known as *Calamagrostis* × *acutiflora*. A particularly upright variety of this hybrid was selected for cultivation purposes and was named *Calamagrostis* × *acutiflora* 'Karl Foerster' after a well-known horticulturalist.

A selection of the best grasses and ferns

The descriptions that follow are given in alphabetical order of botanical names.

The **grasses** are divided into two groups: the **annual** grasses,

◀ *Your choice of grasses may be influenced by their growth habits, the colour and pattern of their leaves, and also the flowers. This particular grass is known as* Miscanthus sinensis *'Kleine Fontäne'.*

Key to symbols

The symbols used in this chapter provide brief information on the flowering season, growth height and light requirements for each plant.

Flowering season

✿ **3–6**

The numbers represent the months of the flowering season.

Growth height

↑ **20–40 (8–16)**

The numbers give the average height in centimetres (inches in brackets), which can vary according to climate and position.

↑ **30/70 (12/28)**

In the case of grasses, a slash is used to distinguish between the height of the foliage (30 cm or 12 in) and that of the flower stems (70 cm or 28 in).

Light requirements

○ The plant prefers a sunny position.

◑ The plant needs light shade or half-shade.

● The plant is shade-tolerant.

Summary of perennial grasses

Giant grasses (up to 180 cm/6 ft)	Sunny positions ○
Arundo donax	Giant reed
Miscanthus × giganteus	
Miscanthus sinensis varieties	Eulalia grass
Cortaderia selloana	Pampas grass

Tall grasses (over 100 cm/40 in)	Sunny positions ○
Calamagrostis × acutiflora 'Karl Foerster'	Feather reed grass
Miscanthus sinensis varieties	Eulalia grass
Panicum virgatum	Switch grass
Phalaris arundinacea 'Picta'	Gardener's garters
Schizachyrium scoparium	Blue stem, wire grass
Spartina pectinata 'Aureomarginata'	
Sorghastrum nutans	India grass
Spodiopogon sibiricus	
Stipa gigantea	Golden oats

Tall grasses (over 100 cm/40 in)	Light to half-shade ◑
Molinia caerulea arundinacea	Tall moor grass

Medium-size grasses (over 40 cm/16 in)	Sunny positions ○
Calamagrostis brachytricha	Korean feather reed grass
Carex buchananii	Leatherleaf sedge
Festuca mairei	
Glyceria maxima var. *variegata*	Striped reed grass
Helictotrichon sempervirens	Blue oat grass
Hystrix patula	Bottlebrush grass
Koeleria glauca	Blue hair grass
Pennisetum alopecuroides	Chinese fountain grass
Sporobolus heterolepis 'Wisconsin Strain'	
Stipa calamagrostis	
Stipa capillata	
Stipa pulcherrima nudicostata	

which like sunflowers are grown from seed and die after flowering; and **herbaceous perennials**. The **bamboos** are effectively a third group, which may be described as perennial grasses with woody stems.

The **ferns**, on the other hand, are a separate group altogether, because although counted as herbaceous perennials they have no flowers.

Many grasses are prized for their decorative leaves, whose long, narrow shapes make for pleasing contrasts.

Ferns are of interest for their foliage alone. The fronds, which are usually compound, are particularly attractive during their initial growth phase.

The most beautiful perennial grasses

Perennial grasses reveal an enormous variety in size and growth habit. Their requirements are also extremely varied with regard to location. To provide some initial help with choosing the right plants, the grasses given in the summary tables on these pages are grouped on the basis of their height and light requirements. This means that you should be able to find a suitable grass for most kinds of perennial bed.

Summary of perennial grasses

Medium-size grasses (over 40 cm/16 in)	Light to half-shade ◗
Carex grayi	Mace sedge
Carex pendula	Pendulous sedge
Carex muskingumensis	Palm-leaf sedge
Chasmanthium latifolium	Spangle grass
Deschampsia cespitosa	Tufted hair grass
Hakonechloa macra 'Aureola'	
Milium effusum 'Aureum'	Golden millet
Molinia caerulea caerulea	Purple moor grass
Luzula sylvatica	Greater woodrush

Low-growing grasses (less than 100 cm/40 in)	Sunny positions ○
Bouteloua gracilis	Mosquito grass
Briza media	Common quaking grass
Carex montana	
Festuca amethystina	
Festuca gautieri	
Festuca glauca	Blue fescue
Festuca ovina	Sheep's fescue
Imperata cylindrica 'Rubra'	Japanese blood grass
Melica ciliata	
Sesleria autumnalis	

Low-growing grasses (less than 40 cm/16 in)	Light to half-shade ◗
Carex elata 'Aurea'	Bowles' golden sedge
Carex morrowii 'Variegata'	
Carex ornithopoda 'Variegata'	
Carex oshimensis 'Evergold'	
Carex plantaginea	
Carex remota	
Carex sylvatica	
Luzula nivea	Snowy woodrush

Arundo donax *(giant reed)*

Giant reed
Arundo donax

EXOTIC-LOOKING SOLITARY GRASS

❀ 8–9 ○

↥ 300/400 (120/160)

Habit: reed-like, upright, spreads by means of running rhizomes.

Leaves: green, broad lanceolate, reed-like, late-sprouting.

Flowers: dense panicles of reddish, later whitish-coloured flowers, which only appear reliably in southern Europe.

Position: medium to damp, nutrient-rich soils in a warm, sunny position; sensitive to winter damp.

Treatment: protection required in harsher locations; cut back in the autumn to provide a layer of leaf mulch; plenty of water and nutrients during the growing season.

Use: solitary grass for mild, sheltered locations; next to walls or in the vicinity of water; the tallest herbaceous grass to be grown in our climate.

Tried-and-tested variety:

• *A. d.* var. *versicolor*: white-striped leaves growing to 200 cm (80 in); much less hardy than the species, so best used as a tub plant and kept frost-free in winter; forms highly ornamental structures.

Mosquito grass
Bouteloua gracilis

ORNAMENTAL GRASS WITH UNUSUAL SEED HEADS

❀ 7–9 ○

↥ 20/40 (8/16)

Habit: clump-forming with upright flower stems.

Leaves: bluish green, narrow lineal, arching, purplish-brown autumn colouring.

Flowers: decorative stems with dark horizontal spikelets that are reminiscent of pods or mosquitoes.

Position: sunny, dry, porous soils without too many nutrients; fond of heat and sensitive to damp; only achieves its full beauty in warm, dry situations.

Treatment: winter protection with leaf mulch recommended in harsher locations.

Use: steppe-like beds and natural-looking plantings in combination with species perennials.

Bouteloua gracilis *(mosquito grass)*

Briza media *(common quaking grass)*

Common quaking grass
Briza media

ORNAMENTAL GRASS WITH
DELICATE FLOWERS

❀ 5–8 ○

↕ 25/40 (10/16)

Habit: forms loose clumps and short runners.

Leaves: narrow, fresh green.

Flowers: large panicles of heart-shaped, brownish-purple spike-lets that tremble in the breeze.

Position: sunny, dryish soils without too many nutrients.

Treatment: no fertilisers; cut out flower panicles when they are no longer attractive; don't cut back tussocks until spring.

Use: for heather, steppe, rock or wildflower gardens, or dry lawns; good for bunches of dried plants.

Tried-and-tested variety:

• **'Limouzi':** larger than the species in all respects – 50/80 cm (20/32 in).

Feather reed grass
Calamagrostis × acutiflora
'Karl Foerster'

LONG-LASTING ORNAMENTAL
WITH A DISTINCTIVE STRUCTURE

❀ 6–8 ○–◑

↕ 60/160 (24/64)

Habit: dense leaf tussocks with stiff, upright flower stems.

Leaves: fresh green, lineal, upright, early-sprouting; bright ochre-yellow autumn colouring from September.

Flowers: narrow, stiffly upright spikes that turn ochre-yellow in high summer.

Position: damp to moderately dry garden soils in sun or half-shade; tolerates heat and short-term dryness; very undemanding with respect to soil and moisture.

Treatment: cut back in late winter to make way for March

growth; too much shade or too many nutrients may lead to weak growth.

Use: versatile; adds structure to borders, open hedgerows and wildflower gardens.

Tried-and-tested variety:

• **'Overdam':** white-edged leaves, stiffly upright, flowers July–September, 50/150 cm (20/60 in); cut back drastical-ly after flowering to produce new growth that is less stiffly upright.

Calamagrostis × acutiflora *'Karl Foerster'*

Calamagrostis brachytricha *(Korean feather reed grass)*

Korean feather reed grass
Calamagrostis brachytricha
(syn. *C. arundinacea* var.
***brachytricha*)**

ATTRACTIVE GRASS ONLY
RECENTLY INTRODUCED INTO
GARDENS

✿ 8–10 ◐–◑

⬆ 60/100 (24/40)

Habit: forms hemispherical clumps with numerous flower stems that project in all directions.

Leaves: dark green, shiny, narrow lanceolate, elegantly arching.

Flowers: silvery pink, borne on finely divided panicles, where raindrops or dew sparkle like diamonds.

Position: open, nutrient-rich soils in sun to half-shade.

Treatment: cut back in spring.

Use: singly or in small groups, to provide structure to borders, wildflower gardens or open hedgerows.

Leatherleaf sedge
Carex buchananii

ORNAMENTAL SEDGE WITH
UNUSUAL COLOURS

✿ 6–7 ◯

⬆ 40/50 (16/20)

Habit: tussock-like clumps.

Leaves: red-brown almost all year round, very narrow, turned over at the tips.

Flowers: each flower stem bears four to five ochre-yellow spikes that scarcely protrude from the leaves and provide no extra decorative value.

Position: damp, open soils in sunny positions; undemanding with regard to soils.

Treatment: looks beautiful in the winter, so leave pruning until spring; winter protection may be needed in exposed locations.

Use: unusual colouring of great interest but difficult to use with other colours; works well with the red foliage of *Heuchera*, red flowers of *Monarda* (bergamot) or red-burred carpets of *Acaena*.

Similar species:

- *C. comans* 'Bronze': sedge from New Zealand; tussocks of long, narrow, bronze-coloured leaves, gently arching; similar treatment to *C. buchananii*; 30/40 cm (12/16 in).

- *C. comans* 'Frosted Curls': dense clumps of golden-bronze leaves; 30/40 cm (12/16 in).

Bowles' golden sedge
Carex elata 'Aurea'

VALUABLE GOLDEN
ORNAMENTAL GRASS

❀ 4–5 ◑

⬆ 40/50 (16/20)

Habit: forms dense clumps.

Leaves: golden-yellow leaves with green edges; colours particularly intense during sprouting; narrow, gently arching, early sprouting, evergreen.

Carex elata *'Aurea' (Bowles' golden sedge)*

Flowers: dense, brownish spikes of little decorative value.

Position: damp, humus-rich soils in light to half-shade; sunny positions only feasible with moist enough soils.

Treatment: don't cut back until spring; water in dry periods.

Use: an interesting grass for brightening up shady woodland margins; particularly effective against a dark background; combines well with *Alchemilla mollis* (lady's mantle), *Hosta*, *Pulmonaria* or *Symphytum* (comfrey).

Mace sedge
Carex grayi

UNDEMANDING GRASS WITH
INTERESTING SEED HEADS

❀ 6–8 ◯–◑

⬆ 50/60 (20/24)

Habit: upright, clump-forming.

Leaves: fresh green, narrow, generally stiff but arching, early-sprouting, remaining green well into autumn.

Flowers: striking-looking star-like spikes.

Position: very undemanding, growing in all garden soils from

Carex grayi *(mace sedge)*

damp to dry; even tolerates parched soil or shallow water; sun to half-shade.

Treatment: cut back early in spring; water during dry periods.

Use: in wildflower gardens, on water banks or by ponds; seed heads good for bunches of dried plants.

Carex montana

GRASS THAT KEEPS ITS
ATTRACTIVENESS

❀ 3–4 ◯

⬆ 15/25 (6/10)

Habit: dense tussocks.

Some fascinating grasses can be found in the many gardens open to the public all over the country, some of them only for short periods in aid of various charities. Details of the latter can be found in the 'yellow book', *Gardens of England and Wales*, published annually by the National Gardens Scheme and available in most good bookshops.

Leaves: fresh green, long and narrow, very early-sprouting; golden-brown autumn colouring.

Flowers: sulphur-yellow flowers like brushes; early-flowering.

Carex morrowii *'Variegata'*

Position: dry to medium soils rich in lime and loam; sun to light shade; likes warmth.

Treatment: cut back in spring; rejuvenate clumps if the grass starts to die off in the middle.

Use: steppe gardens, dry-stone walls, rock gardens, sunny hedgerows.

Carex morrowii 'Variegata'

RELIABLE EVERGREEN GRASS

❀ 4 ◐–◑

↕ 30/40 (12/16)

Habit: dense, hemispherical clumps that grow very large with time.

Leaves: dark green with narrow, creamy-white striped edges; broad lineal; stiffly upright at first but loosely arching later; evergreen, providing year-round interest.

Flowers: tiny yellow spikelets that scarcely emerge from leaves.

Position: damp, humus-rich soils; sun to half-shade; sensitive to excessive dryness and wetness; sunny positions are only feasible where the soil is moist enough, and even then there may be problems with winter frosts.

Treatment: remove unsightly leaves in spring; cut back completely if the whole clump turns brown (it grows back readily); water during dry periods.

Use: in small groups, as underplanting for shrubs, in rhododendron gardens, in the shade of walls; good for shady gardens in combination with *Hosta*, *Pulmonaria*, *Epimedium* or *Tiarella*.

Closely related variety:

• *C.* 'Ice Dance': cream-striped leaves more striking than in *C. morrowii* 'Variegata'; evergreen; forms runners; 30/40 cm (12/16 in).

Carex muskingumensis *(palm-leaf sedge)*

Palm-leaf sedge
Carex muskingumensis

ERECT GRASS OF GREAT INDIVIDUALITY

❁ 7–8 ◯–◗

⬆ 60/70 (24/28)

Habit: thick clumps.

Leaves: fresh green; upright stems covered with narrow lanceolate leaves; reminiscent of palm fronds.

Flowers: short brown terminal spikes.

Position: damp soils rich in humus and loam; sun to half-shade.

Treatment: older clumps often weak, so rejuvenate regularly; varieties often sturdier.

Use: banks and hedgerows.

Tried-and-tested varieties:

• **'Silberstreif'**: green leaves with white stripes; weaker-growing than the species; 50/60 cm (20–24 in).

• **'Wachtposten'**: similar to species but sturdier.

Carex ornithopoda
'Variegata'

WHITE-VARIEGATED DWARF GRASS

❁ 6–7 ◗

⬆ 15/20 (6/8)

Habit: dense clumps.

Leaves: fresh green with white stripes, narrow lineal, arching, evergreen.

Flowers: decorative spikes, bent like claws and grouped together to resemble birds' toes.

Position: open, humus-rich soils; light to half-shade; likes warmth and lime.

Treatment: don't cut back until spring.

Use: in small groups, providing leaf and colour contrast with shade or half-shade plants such as *Hosta*, *Heuchera* or *Pulmonaria*.

Carex oshimensis 'Evergold' (syn. *C. hachijoensis* 'Evergold')

VALUABLE DWARF GRASS

❁ 4–5 ◖–●

⬆ 20/30 (8/12)

Habit: decorative clumps.

Leaves: fresh green with striking yellow medial stripe; very narrow; evergreen.

Flowers: thin flower stems with tiny spikes; of no decorative value.

Position: open, humus-rich soils; provides lasting beauty in sheltered shady or half-shaded areas.

Treatment: remove unsightly leaves after the winter, cutting

Carex oshimensis *'Evergold'*

Most grasses are at their best in summer because their leaves die back in the winter, but there are many evergreen kinds that look equally attractive in winter. Most grasses should not be cut back until the spring.

back completely if necessary; protection from frost and winter sun is recommended.

Use: in small groups; good for brightening up shrubberies and hedgerows; in courtyards or in the shade of walls.

Similar species:

• *C. conica* 'Snowline': shallow, disparate clumps; long, narrow lanceolate leaves, dark green with white edges; evergreen; 15/20 cm (6/8 in); use and treatment similar to *C. oshimensis* 'Evergold'.

Pendulous sedge
Carex pendula

LONG-LASTING, EVERGREEN
SOLITARY GRASS

❀ 5–6 ◑–●

↕ 50/100 (20/40)

Habit: impressively broad, bushy clumps.

Leaves: shiny, dark green, broad lineal, arching, evergreen.

Flowers: graceful flower stems with hanging spikes, projecting well beyond the leaves.

Position: damp soils rich in humus and loam but poor in lime; half to full shade; generally undemanding; sunny positions only feasible with sufficiently moist soil, but then there are problems with winter frosts.

Treatment: prune unsightly clumps in the spring or even cut them back completely (they will grow back readily); spreads by self-seeding, so remove unwanted seedlings; allow plenty of space.

Carex plantaginea

Use: plant either singly or in groups, as underplanting for shrubs, in wildflower gardens or in shady gardens; *C. pendula* works well in combination with other, similarly vigorous shade perennials such as *Rodgersia*, *Hosta* or *Aruncus dioicus* (goatsbeard).

Carex plantaginea

ATTRACTIVE ORNAMENTAL
FOLIAGE PLANT

❀ 5–6 ◑–●

↕ 20/30 (8/12)

Habit: forms broad, shallow clumps, and spreads by means of short runners to form extensive carpets over time.

Leaves: dark green, broad lineal, lots of veins, evergreen.

Flowers: narrow, light-yellow spikes.

Position: dry to medium soils, rich in humus and loam, in shade or half-shade; sensitive to wetness; frost problems in sunny positions.

Treatment: cut back in spring.

Use: pretty foliage plant for shade or half-shade; small groups contrast nicely with *Pulmonaria, Hosta, Tiarella, Epimedium* or ferns.

Similar species:

* **C. siderosticha** 'Variegata': broad-leaved white-variegated sedge, quite similar to *C. plantaginea* but with noticeable white stripes and not evergreen; 20/30 cm (8/12 in); similar requirements to *C. plantaginea*.

Carex pseudocyperus

VIGOROUS GRASS FOR WATER GARDENS

❀ 6–9 ○–◗

↑ 40/80 (16/32)

Habit: loose clumps, spreading to form lawns.

Leaves: dark green, broad lanceolate, with sharp edges, gently arching.

Flowers: triangular flower stems with nodding flower heads made up of green (later straw-coloured) cylindrical spikes on long stalks; good for bunches of dried plants.

Position: damp, waterlogged or even flooded soils rich in nutrients and lime in warm situations; sun to half-shade.

Treatment: the species self-seeds and proliferates some-what, so plant in a container if space is limited.

Use: marsh beds, shallow water gardens (depth 10–30 cm/4–12 in), river banks or the edges of ponds.

Carex remota

HIGHLY DECORATIVE NATIVE GRASS

❀ 5–7 ◖–●

↑ 40/45 (16/18)

Habit: tussock-forming.

Leaves: fresh green, very narrow, arching.

Flowers: tiny spikes, mainly at the end of arching flower stems.

Carex pseudocyperus

Position: damp to wet soils rich in humus and loam; half to full shade.

Treatment: after flowering, gather in tussocks and cut back flower stems to prevent seeding.

Use: the pretty tussocks make for dramatic contrasts if you plant them between shade or half-shade perennials such as *Bergenia, Helleborus foetidus* (stinking hellebore), *Euphorbia amygdaloides* 'Purpurea', *Alchemilla mollis* (lady's mantle) or ferns.

23

Chasmanthium latifolium *(spangle grass)*

Similar species:

- *C. caryophyllea*: interesting sedge with dense, broad tussocks of long, very narrow, dark-green leaves; flowers March–April; 20/35 cm (8/14 in); vigorous and adaptable; requirements and use similar to *C. remota*.

Cortaderia is dioecious, which means it has male and female flowers on separate plants. The female plants are more popular because their flowers are more attractive.

Carex sylvatica

NATIVE GRASS FOR SHADE

❀ 5–6   ◖–●

↑ 40/70 (16/28)

Habit: loose clumps.

Leaves: shiny, dark green, broad lineal, arching, evergreen.

Flowers: nodding ears on gently arching stems.

Position: damp, nutrient-rich soils with plenty of humus and loam; half to full shade.

Treatment: self-seeds without becoming a problem; tidy up winter-damaged clumps, cutting them right back if severely damaged; they quickly regenerate.

Use: in open woodland or hedgerows, in combination with shade perennials or ferns, or as underplanting for shrubs.

Spangle grass
Chasmanthium latifolium (syn. *Uniola latifolia*)

ORNAMENTAL GRASS WITH CONSPICUOUS SEED HEADS

❀ 8–10   ◖–●

↑ 70/100 (18/40)

Habit: upright, in loose clumps.

Leaves: fresh green, broad lineal, late-sprouting; flower stems covered in leaves; glorious autumn colouring.

Flowers: loose terminal panicles of flattened greenish spikes that turn yellowish after flowering.

Position: damp, nutrient-rich soils, preferably with plenty of loam; sunny; likes warmth.

Treatment: cut back in spring.

Use: by ponds, in damp borders, along hedgerows; singly or in groups; good for bunches of dried plants.

Pampas grass
Cortaderia selloana

IMPRESSIVE SOLITARY GRASS

❀ 9–10   ○

↑ 80/250 (32/100)

Habit: leaf tussocks dominated by towering flower stems.

Leaves: grey-green, narrow lineal, elegantly arching, evergreen.

Flowers: feathery, silvery-white panicles on tall stems.

Position: open, nutrient-rich soils in warm, sunny situations.

Treatment: should only be planted in spring; needs plenty of moisture in summer, but keep as dry as possible in winter (sensitive to wetness); one method is to gather the leaf tussocks together and tie them up with dry leaves and brush-wood (see page 83); don't cut back until spring.

Use: solitary grass for borders and next to walls.

Tried-and-tested varieties:

- **'Pumila':** 50/120 (20/50 in); compact, silvery-white panicles.
- **'Sunningdale Silver':** 80/250 cm (32/100 in); loose, shiny, silvery flower panicles; the most impressive yet the most elegant variety.

Tufted hair grass
Deschampsia cespitosa

NATIVE GRASS FOR HEDGEROWS

❀ 6–8 ◑–●

↑ 30/100 (12/40)

Habit: hemispherical tussocks.

Leaves: dark green, rough-textured, narrow lineal, early-sprouting.

Flowers: large, cloud-like flower heads on tall stems; golden-yellow autumn colours.

Position: damp soils rich in humus and loam; light to half-shade; sunny positions too if sufficient moisture is present; generally undemanding.

Treatment: don't cut back until spring; species plants self-seed profusely, so varieties are more suitable for gardens.

Use: wildflower gardens, hedgerows, meadows, in front of dark shrubs.

Tried-and-tested varieties:

- **'Golden Pendant':** arching golden-yellow flower pani-cles; 50/100 cm (20/40 in).
- **'Golden Veil':** upright flower stems with silvery-green pani-cles that later turn golden-yellow; 40/90 cm (16/36 in).
- **'Tauträger':** attractive flower panicles; late-flowering (August); 40/90 cm (16/36 in).

Cotton grass
Eriophorum latifolium

CLUMP-FORMING GRASS WITH CONSPICUOUS SEED HEADS

❀ 4–6 ○

↑ 40/60 (16/24)

Habit: long-lasting clumps.

Leaves: fresh green, flat, lanceolate.

Cortaderia selloana *'Sunningdale Silver'*

Deschampsia cespitosa *'Tauträger'*

Flowers: insignificant flowers give way to tufts of woolly, silky-white seed heads.

Position: damp, wet or even waterlogged soils (water up to 5 cm/2 in deep), boggy and poor in nutrients; sunny.

Treatment: straightforward.

Use: bogs or marshes, pond margins, shallow ponds; seed heads good with dried plants.

Similar species:

• **E. angustifolium:** narrower leaves; proliferates by means of runners; weak-flowering; only suitable for water gardens; 30/40 cm (12/16 in).

Festuca glauca *'Azurit'*

Festuca amethystina

 6–7 ○

↑ 30/50 (12/20)

Habit: shallow clumps.

Leaves: blue-green, fine, almost needle-like, slightly arching, evergreen.

Flowers: loose, drooping spikes; in summer, the leaves and flower stems display a variety of coppery or violet tints that create a rainbow effect.

Position: open, dry to medium soils; warm and sunny.

Treatment: don't cut back until spring; remove wilted flowers.

Use: wildflower gardens, gravel gardens, steppe gardens.

Festuca gautieri (syn. *F. scoparia*)

CUSHION-FORMING DWARF GRASS

 6–7 ○–◑

↑ 15/25 (6/10)

Habit: hemispherical clumps, developing into dense cushions.

Leaves: fresh green, needle-like, stiff, rather erect, evergreen.

Flowers: yellowish-green panicles that float like a veil above the leaves and quickly turn yellow.

Position: open, moderately dry soils poor in nutrients; sun to half-shade; only thrives on poor soils; avoid winter sun.

Treatment: allow plenty of space (crowded cushions wilt very early); cut back and rejuvenate cushions that are balding in the centre.

Use: not as ground cover but either singly or in small groups in steppe gardens, heather gardens or miniature gardens.

Tried-and-tested variety:

• **'Pic Carlit':** more decorative and compact than the species; fresh green; 10/15 cm (4/6 in)

Blue fescue *Festuca glauca* (syn. *F. cinerea*)

DWARF GRASS WITH MANY VARIETIES

 6–7 ○

↑ 30/40 (12/24)

Habit: hedgehog-like cushions of leaves.

Leaves: grey-blue, fine, narrow lineal.

Flowers: loose blue-green panicles that quickly turn yellow.

Position: open soils that are poor in both humus and nutrients; warm locations in full sun; tolerates heat and dryness; damp or nutrient-rich soils make the grass greener and also shorten its life; blue colouring strongest in plants grown on poor soil.

Treatment: remove flowers as soon as they turn yellow, to retain beauty of plant.

Use: singly or in small groups, in steppe gardens, gravel gardens, rock gardens or miniature gardens.

Tried-and-tested varieties:

- **'Azurit':** silvery blue; 20/40 cm (8/16 in).
- **'Blaufink':** silvery blue; 25/60 cm (10/24 in).
- **'Blue Fox'** (syn. 'Blaufuchs'): steel-blue, lasting into autumn; 15/25 cm (6/10 in).
- **'Frühlingsblau':** grey-blue; 25/40 cm (10/16 in).
- **'Harz':** blue-green.
- **'Meerblau':** steel-blue; 25/60 cm (10/24 in).
- **'Seeigel':** sea-green.

Festuca mairei

Festuca mairei

TUSSOCK GRASS FORMING INTERESTING PATTERNS

❀ 6–7 ○

↑ 50/100 (20/40)

Habit: dense clumps.

Leaves: grey-green, narrow lineal, sharp edges, arching.

Flowers: elegantly arching panicles, early-flowering, but fading and yellowing in the summer.

Position: open, moderately dry, sandy loams; sunny situations.

Treatment: has beautiful autumn and winter colours, so don't cut back until spring.

Festuca gautieri *syn.* F. scoparia

Glyceria maxima *var.* variegata *(striped reed grass)*

Use: solitary grass, singly or in groups, in steppe gardens, wildflower gardens, on sunny banks or patios.

Sheep's fescue
Festuca ovina

HEMISPHERICAL DWARF GRASS

❀ 6–7 ○

⬆ 20/30 (8/12)

Habit: dense, hemispherical clumps, with radiating stems.

Leaves: green to grey-green, narrow lineal, stiffly upright, early-sprouting.

Flowers: narrow, green panicles that become unsightly after flowering.

Position: open, dry soils poor in nutrients; warm and sunny; poor soils prolong its life, while overfed clumps age quickly.

Treatment: remove flowers when they become unsightly; when clumps go bald in the centre, divide to rejuvenate.

Use: steppe gardens, heather gardens, rock gardens, miniature gardens.

Tried-and-tested variety:

• 'Solling': grey-green.

Striped reed grass
Glyceria maxima var. *variegata*

VIGOROUS WHITE-VARIEGATED GRASS

❀ 7–8 ○

⬆ 60/80 (24/32)

Habit: proliferates by means of runners.

Leaves: green and yellowish-white stripes, with green edges; new growth has whitish and reddish tints.

Flowers: upright stems topped with finely divided panicles.

Position: damp garden soils; also next to water or in boggy areas with up to 15 cm (6 in) of water; sunny.

Treatment: watch for proliferation and keep in check; best for larger ponds; in smaller ponds, plant in containers.

Use: versatile plant that thrives as vigorously in ordinary garden soils as in shallow water.

Hakonechloa macra 'Aureola'

ORNAMENTAL GRASS WITH LOVELY YELLOW VARIEGATION

✿ 8–10 ◑

↑ 40/45 (16/18)

Habit: tussocks that spread slowly by means of short runners.

Leaves: bright yellow-and-green stripes, lineal, elegantly arching, reddish tints in new growth and autumn colouring.

Flowers: loose golden-yellow panicles growing only just clear of the leaves.

Hakonechloa macra *'Aureola'*

Position: open, damp soils rich in humus and nutrients; light to half-shade; sunny in cool climates; turns green with increasing shade.

Treatment: winter protection needed in harsher locations; don't cut back until spring.

Use: underplanting for shrubs; creates nice colour contrasts with *Heuchera*, *Bergenia* and *Alchemilla mollis* (lady's mantle).

Blue oat grass
Helictotrichon sempervirens

TALLEST BLUE-TINTED ORNAMENTAL GRASS

✿ 8–10 ○

↑ 50/120 (20/48)

Habit: radiating clumps.

Leaves: bluish grey, narrow, early-sprouting, evergreen.

Flowers: loose, yellowish-brown panicles on tall stems.

Position: open, dry to moder-ately dry soils poor in nutrients; full sun; tolerates heat.

Treatment: long-lived in poor soils; shade and rich soils cause the leaves to turn green and encourage fungal infection; dry

Helictotrichon sempervirens *'Saphirsprudel'*

flower stems can be removed in the summer as soon as they start to become unsightly, but you shouldn't cut back fully until spring.

Use: in dry beds and borders together with other blue- or silvery-leaved perennials such as *Iris barbata* hybrids, *Nepeta* (catmint), *Lavandula* (laven-der) or *Stachys byzantina* (lamb's tongue).

Tried-and-tested variety:

- 'Saphirsprudel': blue-green; less vulnerable to fungal infection than species.

29

Hystrix patula *(bottlebrush grass)*

Bottlebrush grass
Hystrix patula

STEPPE GRASS WITH STRIKING-
LOOKING SEED HEADS

 6–8 ○

 50/90 (20/36)

Habit: loose clumps, stiffly upright, weak-growing.

Leaves: arching, reed-like leaves borne on fresh-green, upright stems.

Flowers: whitish green, later brownish; loose spikes with stiff bristles, reminiscent of bottle-brushes.

Position: moderately dry to normal, sandy soils rich in humus or loam, sunny; sensitive to winter damp.

Treatment: species usually short-lived but self-seeds well in favourable conditions.

Use: heather or steppe gardens, meadows; also makes a good dried plant.

Japanese blood grass
Imperata cylindrica 'Rubra' (syn. 'Red Baron')

DWARF GRASS WITH INTENSE RED COLOURING

 ○

30–40 (12–16)

Habit: loose clumps, spreads slowly by means of short runners.

Leaves: fresh green, narrow lineal, turning bright red through the summer.

Flowers: doesn't flower in Europe.

Position: nutrient-rich soils, sunny; likes warmth; can be grown in light shade, but red colouring will be reduced.

Treatment: winter protection required in cold areas, preferably with dry leaves and brushwood.

Use: provides red colours in perennial borders; sunny hedgerows (though not too dry); can be very effective as a tub plant.

Imperata cylindrica *'Rubra' (Japanese blood grass)*

Juncus effusus *'Spiralis' (corkscrew rush)*

Corkscrew rush
Juncus effusus 'Spiralis'

RUSH WITH SPIRAL STEMS

❀ 6–8 ◐–◑

↕ 40/60 (16/24)

Habit: compact, bushy clumps.

Stem: shiny, yellowish-green, corkscrew-shaped.

Flowers: small, drooping brown flowers, grouped in tufts.

Position: damp to wet soils rich in nutrients and poor in lime; tolerates 5–10 cm (2–4 in) of standing water.

Treatment: very little required.

Use: marsh beds, pond edges, shallow water.

Other species:

- *J. ensifolius*: lawn-like growth; 20/30 cm (8/12 in).
- *J. inflexus* (hard rush): blue-green rush that forms dense cushions; 50/60 cm (20/24 in).

Blue hair grass
Koeleria glauca

HEDGEHOG-LIKE TUSSOCK GRASS FOR BARREN POSITIONS

❀ 6–7 ◯

↕ 15/25 (6/10)

Habit: bushy clumps.

Leaves: blue-green, narrow lineal; onion-like swellings at base of stems; leaves often wilt after flowering, but soon sprout again after a short rest.

Flowers: dense, brownish-green spikes in profusion (though not every year).

Position: open, dry, sandy soils poor in nutrients; lime-rich soils OK too; short-lived in nutrient-rich soils due to exhaustion from too much flowering.

Treatment: don't cut back until spring.

Use: rock, heather, steppe or gravel gardens.

Snowy woodrush
Luzula nivea

EVERGREEN GRASS FOR SHADE

❀ 6–7 ◐–●

↕ 20/40 (8/16)

Habit: loose clumps, lawn-like development.

Leaves: dark green, narrow lineal, hairy, arching, evergreen.

Flowers: white, grouped in tufts, on tall stems.

Position: soils rich in humus and loam; light to half-shade.

Treatment: don't cut back until spring; check for proliferation, and if necessary reduce this.

Use: tolerates shade and root pressure; shady wildflower gardens, hedgerows, underplanting for shrubs, shade gardens.

Luzula nivea *(snowy woodrush)*

Luzula sylvatica *(greater woodrush)*

Greater woodrush
Luzula sylvatica

STRONG GRASS FOR PLANTING
AROUND SHRUBS

 4–5 ◐–●

↕ 30/80 (12/32)

Habit: loose clumps, spreads by means of short runners to form lawn-like carpets.

Leaves: shiny, dark green, hairy edges, evergreen, early-sprouting.

Flowers: brown spikes on branching stems.

Position: damp, humus-rich soils; light to full shade; evergreen in cool, damp positions if protected from winter sun.

Treatment: cut back in spring if leaves damaged over winter; check for proliferation and if necessary curb it.

Use: tolerates shade and pressure from roots; hedgerows, underplanting for shrubs; intersperse with equally vigorous ferns and shade perennials.

Tried-and-tested varieties:

- **'Hohe Tatra':** taller and stronger than species; fresh green; in upright rosettes; 40/90 cm (16/36 in).

- **'Marginata':** silvery-edged leaves; 20/40 cm (8/16 in).

- **'Tauernpass':** fresh green; not as tall as species; forms broad, shallow leaf rosettes; 20/40 cm (8/16 in).

- **'Wintergold':** intense gold colouring; 20/40 cm (8/16 in).

Melica ciliata

MELICK GRASS FOR DRY,
SUNNY POSITIONS

5–6 ○

↕ 30/60 (12/24)

Habit: loose clumps.

Leaves: grey-green, narrow lanceolate, usually curled, stiff upright.

Flowers: dense, cylindrical panicles of silvery spikes, turning pale yellow; long-lasting.

Position: dry, open, gravelly soils rich in lime; sunny and warm; floppy growth in damp positions.

Treatment: keep more vigorous plants well apart.

Melica ciliata

Use: heather, rock, steppe or wildflower gardens.

Golden millet
Milium effusum 'Aureum'

NATIVE GRASS FOR SHADY WOODLANDS

 5–6 ◐–●

🡹 30/80 (12/32)

Habit: loose clumps, develops short runners.

Leaves: golden yellow, particularly intense during sprouting; lineal, arching.

Flowers: loose, golden-yellow panicles, turned over at the tips and fluttering in the breeze.

Position: open, damp, nutritious soils with plenty of humus and loam; shade; shallow roots.

Treatment: self-seeds, but seedlings should be removed as they are less colourful.

Use: makes a beautiful splash of colour in the shade, creating dramatic leaf and colour contrasts with *Heuchera*, *Euphorbia amygdaloides* 'Purpurea', *Helleborus foetidus* (stinking hellebore), *Bergenia* and ferns; tolerant of root pressure, so makes good underplanting for shrubs.

Miscanthus × *giganteus* (syn. *M. florindulus*, *M. japonicus*)

REED-LIKE SOLITARY GRASS

✿ 10–11 ○

🡹 300/400 (120/160)

Habit: upright, reed-like, spreading slowly by means of short runners to produce broad clumps.

Leaves: arching, bluish green foliage on stiffly upright stems; late-sprouting, turning into impressive ochre-yellow autumn colouring.

Flowers: silvery-grey, feathery panicles, only appearing after long, warm summers when there has been sufficient moisture present.

Position: damp, nutrient-rich soils; sunny and warm.

Treatment: don't prune until spring as the plant retains its beauty through the winter; feed regularly.

Use: this solitary grass makes an excellent backdrop for other plants, but is not suitable as a hedge plant or for dividing parts of the garden, because it doesn't reach its full height until summer.

Miscanthus × giganteus

There are probably more cultivated varieties of *Miscanthus sinensis* (eulalia grass) than of any other grass species. The reason for this lies in the many different purposes for which this grass has been developed. Varieties have been selected for their decorative flowers, for their height, for their attractive leaves and for their autumn colouring.

Miscanthus sinensis (eulalia grass) comes in many different varieties.

Eulalia grass
Miscanthus sinensis

HIGHLY ORNAMENTAL GRASS
WITH MANY VARIETIES

✿ 8–10 ○

↑ 80–250/100–300
(32–100/40–120)

Habit: the stiffly upright, reed-like clumps expand with time by means of short runners.

Leaves: dark green, usually with a silver stripe along the centre; broad lineal, arching; many varieties with gorgeous autumn colouring.

Flowers: feathery panicles, varying in colour from silvery or whitish to brownish red, depending on the variety and the degree of ripeness; some varieties rarely if ever come into flower, but are nonetheless valuable as foliage plants.

Position: all damp, nutritious garden soils in warm, sunny situations; generally undemanding.

Treatment: remains attractive through winter, so don't prune until spring; if it self-seeds, remove seedlings to preserve the more valuable varieties.

Use: as a solitary grass on borders or next to water; good for following on other plants later in the year; even the tallest varieties are not suitable as screening plants because they sprout late and don't attain their full height until late summer.

Tried-and-tested varieties:

- **'Gracillimus':** narrow, attractive leaves; doesn't flower; 150–180 cm (60–72 in).

- **'Graziella':** flowers early and reliably (silvery pink); 130/150 cm (52/60 in).

- **'Kleine Fontäne':** silvery-brown flowers appear early; 90/160 cm (36/64 in); see photo on page 12.

- **'Kleine Silberspinne':** early-flowering; very fine leaves with broad silver stripe; 80/140 cm (32/56 in).

- **'Malepartus':** silvery-red flowers; flame-like autumn colouring; 170/200 cm (68/80 in).

- **'Nippon':** bronze-tinted leaves, turning coppery in autumn; 90/150 cm (36/60 in).

- **'Silberspinne':** very fine leaves; flowers profusely; 130/200 cm (52–80 in).

- **'Silver Feather'** (syn. 'Silberfeder'): silvery-white flowers; golden-yellow autumn colouring; 200/240 cm (80/96 in).

- **'Sirene':** red-brown flowers; glorious red-brown autumn colouring; 150/250 cm (60/100 in).

- **'Strictus':** yellow stripes; rarely flowers; stiffly upright; 180/220 cm (72/88 in).

- **'Variegatus':** silvery-striped leaves; 180/200 cm (72/80 in).

- **'Yakushima Dwarf':** narrow leaves; pinkish-brown flowers; 60/100 cm (24/40 in).

• **'Zebrinus'**: yellow stripes; arching leaves; rarely flowers; 180/220 cm (72/88 in).

Tall moor grass
Molinia caerulea arundinacea

EXUBERANT TUSSOCK GRASS

✿ 8–10 ◐–◑

↕ 50–60/180–200 (20–24/72–80)

Habit: tussock-like clumps dominated by towering flower stems.

Leaves: fresh green, narrow lineal, elegantly arching, late-sprouting, with long-lasting gold autumn colouring.

Flowers: loose panicles on leafless stems, turning golden-yellow after flowering.

Position: very adaptable; damp soils; sun to half-shade; tolerates summer or winter dryness.

Treatment: don't cut back until the spring; any seedlings should be removed as they are less valuable than the cultivated varieties.

Use: gives structure to borders; sunny hedgerows, heather gardens, wildflower gardens; combines well with autumn-flowering perennials and shrubs with good autumn colours.

Tried-and-tested varieties:
• **'Karl Foerster'**: tall-growing variety; 50/200 cm (20/80 in).
• **'Transparent'**: loosely arching panicles; very graceful; 50/180 cm (20/72 in)
• **'Windspiel'**: stiffly upright; sturdy; tallest variety; 60/240 cm (24/96 in).

Purple moor grass
Molinia caerulea caerulea

NATIVE GRASS WITH ORNAMENTAL VARIETIES

✿ 8–9 ◐–◑

↕ 30–40/50–120 (12–16/20–48)

Habit: dense clumps dominated by towering flower stems.

Leaves: bluish green, narrow lineal, turned over slightly at the tips, with glorious yellow-brown autumn colouring.

Flowers: thin, brownish panicles on wiry stems, turning bright yellowish-brown after flowering.

Position: damp, humus-rich soils; sun to half-shade; sunny positions only with sufficient moisture.

Treatment: don't cut back until spring, on account of impressive autumn and winter appearance.

Molinia caerulea arundinacea *'Windspiel'*

Use: in small groups in heather or wildflower gardens or open hedgerows; good against a dark background.

Tried-and-tested varieties:
• **'Dauerstrahl'**: radiating clumps; glorious autumn colours; 40/120 cm (16/48 in).
• **'Moorhexe'**: narrow, upright clumps; 30/80 cm (12/32 in).
• **'Strahlenquelle'**: radiating clumps; 40/120 cm (16/80 in).
• **'Variegata'**: yellowish-white striped leaves; 30/50 cm (12/20 in).

Panicum virgatum *'Rotstrahlbusch'*

Switch grass
Panicum virgatum

FASCINATING ORNAMENTAL
GRASS

✿ 8–9 ○

↕ 80/100 (32/40)

Habit: clumps made up of
many upright stems.

Leaves: fresh green, narrow
lineal, elegantly arching, late-
sprouting, with attractive ochre-
yellow autumn colouring.

Flowers: divided panicles of
tiny light-brown scented
spikelets, growing only a short
distance above the leaves.

Position: moderately dry to
damp soils; sunny and warm;
nutrient-rich soils may cause
floppy growth.

Treatment: don't cut back until
spring; long-lasting, easy-care.

Use: sunny borders; goes well
with autumn flowers such as
Michaelmas daisies (*Aster novae-
angliae, A. novi-belgii*), autumn
chrysanthemums (*Chrysanthe-
mum*) or golden rod (*Solidago*);
suitable for use with cut flowers.

Tried-and-tested varieties:

- **'Hänse Herms':** bright
  brownish-red autumn colouring; 60/80 cm (24/32 in).
- **'Heavy Metal':** blue-green
  leaves; stiffly upright; 60/160
  cm (24/64 in).
- **'Rehbraun':** reddish-brown
  autumn colouring; 90/100 cm
  (36/40 in).
- **'Strictum':** more stiffly
  upright than the species;
  60/150 cm (24/60 in).

Chinese fountain grass
Pennisetum alopecuroides

PROFUSELY FLOWERING GRASS

✿ 9–10 ○

↕ 60/80 (24/32)

Habit: hemispherical clumps.

Leaves: grey-green, narrow
lineal, arching, late-sprouting,
golden-yellow autumn
colouring.

Flowers: hosts of spiral-shaped
red-brown spikes like tiny
foxes' tails.

Position: open, moderately dry
to moderately damp soils;
sunny.

Treatment: cut back in spring;
lots of watering in summer
makes for good flowering.

Use: singly or in small groups to
give structure to borders; combines well with autumn foliage
perennials and shrubs; excellen
for linking low-growing perenni
als with dwarf bushes.

Pennisetum alopecuroides *'Compressu*

Phalaris arundinacea *'Picta'*
(gardener's garters)

Tried-and-tested varieties:

- **'Compressum'**: dense clumps; bright-yellow autumn colours; 50/70 cm (20/28 in).

- **'Hameln'**: compact; flowers earlier than species (Aug.–Sept.); 30/60 cm (12/24 in).

- **'Herbstzauber'**: glorious autumn colouring; lots of flowers; 40/50 cm (16/20 in).

- **'Weserbergland'**: lowest-growing variety; 25/40 cm (10/16 in).

Gardener's garters
Phalaris arundinacea 'Picta'

STRONG WHITE-VARIEGATED ORNAMENTAL GRASS

 6–7 ○–◑

↑ 100/120 (40/48)

Habit: proliferates by means of strong runners, forming dense thickets in favourable locations.

Leaves: narrow and reed-like, with green and white stripes; three colours during sprouting (green, white and soft pink).

Flowers: narrow, elongated grey-green panicles, insignificant in comparison with leaves.

Position: damp to wet, nutrient-rich soils; sun to half-shade.

Treatment: water in dry weather; leaves can turn brown in dry summers, but if cut back immediately will regenerate in their former glory; check for proliferation and reduce if necessary.

Use: used mainly for its attractive leaves, which contrast nicely in pattern and colour with large-leaved purple or green perennials and shrubs.

Common reed
Phragmites australis

PROLIFERATING REED FOR WATER GARDENS

✿ 7–9 ○

↑ 200/400 (80/160)

Habit: stiffly upright; proliferates by means of creeping underground rhizomes.

Leaves: blue-green, broad, growing out stiffly from their stems; loss of foliage leaves bare stems through the winter.

Flowers: brownish terminal panicles 20–40 cm (8–16 in) long.

Position: nutrient-rich marsh or water zones; tolerates water up to 1 m (40 in) deep; not suitable for lined ponds as rhizomes may penetrate the lining.

Treatment: keep proliferation in check, planting in containers if necessary.

Use: only recommended for water gardens; good for strengthening river banks.

Tried-and-tested variety:

- **'Variegatus'**: valuable, less invasive variety, recommended for smaller ponds; leaves have bright-yellow stripes, turning greener through the summer; few if any flowers; 120–150 cm (48–60 in).

Grasses for water gardens that are liable to proliferate can be stopped from spreading too rapidly by being planted in containers. The most suitable containers for this are thin plastic pots that can be sunk just out of sight.

Blue stem, wire grass
Schizachyrium scoparium
(syn. *Andropogon scoparius*)

DECORATIVE PRAIRIE GRASS

✿ 8–10 ○

↑ 100/120 (40/48)

Habit: stiffly upright clumps.

Leaves: bluish green, narrow, late-sprouting, glorious reddish-brown autumn colouring.

Schoenoplectus lacustris *(common bulrush)*

Flowers: narrow, brownish panicles that turn reddish-brown after flowering.

Position: open, moderately dry to moderately damp, nutrient-rich soils; warm and sunny.

Treatment: cut back in spring.

Use: gives structure to prairie gardens together with late-summer flowers e.g. Michaelmas daisy (*Aster novi-belgii*, *A. novi-angliae*), black-eyed Susan (*Rudbeckia fulgida* 'Goldsturm'), golden rod (*Solidago*) or cone-flower (*Echinacea purpurea*).

Common bulrush
Schoenoplectus lacustris
(syn. *Scirpus lacustris*)

DECORATIVE WATER PLANT

✿ 6–10 ○

↑ 100–300 (40–120)

Habit: spreads by means of long runners to cover wide areas.

Leaves: elegantly arching, on round, leafless, dark-green stems 100–300 cm (40–120 in) long.

Flowers: dark-brown terminal spikes.

Position: wet pond margins or shallow standing or gently flowing water up to 3 m (10 ft) deep.

Treatment: check for proliferation; in smaller ponds, plant in containers to limit spread.

Use: picturesque habit good for water gardens, with the long stems reflected in the water; river banks or garden ponds.

Tried-and-tested variety:

• **'Albescens':** white stripes along stems; invasive; 100–200 cm (40–80 in).

Sesleria autumnalis

AUTUMN-FLOWERING GRASS OF LONG-LASTING BEAUTY

✿ 9–10 ○–◑

↑ 30/40 (12/16)

Habit: hedgehog-like clumps, developing short runners.

Leaves: light green, narrow and rough-textured, standing upright.

Flowers: tiny, delicate, silvery-white spikes.

Position: open, sandy or gravelly, lime-rich soils; sun to light shade.

Treatment: don't cut back until spring.

Use: decorative all year round; hedgerows, wildflower or steppe gardens.

Sorghastrum nutans *(Indian grass)*

Indian grass
Sorghastrum nutans
(syn. *S. avenaceum*)

BEAUTIFUL GRASS IN THE HIGH
SUMMER

❀ 8–10 ○

↑ 80/150 (32/60)

Habit: large clumps of narrow, stiffly upright stems.

Leaves: grey-green, narrow, late-sprouting, intense brownish-red autumn colouring.

Flowers: dense violet-brown spikes with golden-yellow stamens.

Position: very undemanding; moderately dry to moderately damp garden soils; sunny and warm.

Treatment: don't cut back until spring (retains beauty throughout winter).

Use: sunny borders and steppe gardens in combination with autumn-flowering plants.

Spartina pectinata
'Aureomarginata'

STRIKING ORNAMENTAL GRASS
WITH ELEGANT LINES

❀ 8–9 ○–◑

↑ 130/150 (52/60)

Habit: spreads by means of short runners to form dense thickets; somewhat invasive.

Leaves: fresh green with golden-yellow stripes along the edges; elegantly arching; very

sharp edges; bright-yellow autumn colouring.

Flowers: compact, straw-yellow spikes just above the leaves; not very attractive.

Position: all garden soils; damp or even wet; sun to light shade.

Treatment: cut back in spring; very attractive under frost or snow; full beauty only becomes apparent after three or four years; check for proliferation

Spartina pectinata *'Aureomarginata'*

(unwanted runners can be easily removed if dealt with quickly).

Use: attractive grass for damp borders, river banks and ponds.

Spodiopogon sibiricus

LONG-LASTING ORNAMENTAL

❀ 7–9 ○–◑

↕ 120/160 (48/64)

Habit: dense clumps with stiffly upright flower stems; develops short runners; sturdy.

Leaves: fresh green, short, reed-like, sticking out almost horizontally, with glorious red-brown autumn colouring.

Flowers: loose panicles of bright-purple spikelets.

Position: very adaptable; no particular soils; moderately dry to damp; sun to half-shade; grows best in warm, damp summers.

> *Sporobolus heterolepis* 'Wisconsin Strain' is a profusely flowering variety of the wild species known as the prairie dropseed, which is native to the North American prairies. This new grass variety comes highly recommended.

Treatment: don't cut back until spring.

Use: borders, hedgerows, steppe gardens; valuable grass to accompany cut flowers.

Sporobolus heterolepis 'Wisconsin Strain'

PROFUSELY FLOWERING VARIETY OF PRAIRIE DROPSEED

❀ 8–10 ○

↕ 30/60 (12/24)

Habit: dense clumps with lush veils of flowers.

Leaves: fresh green, very fine, arching, with attractive copper-red autumn colouring.

Flowers: finely divided panicles standing well above the leaves; flowers reliably and well.

Position: moderately dry to fairly damp soils; sunny; likes warmth and tolerates dryness.

Treatment: cut back in spring.

Use: gives structure to prairie plantings in combination with autumn-flowering Michaelmas daisies (*Aster novi-belgii*, *A. ericoides*), black-eyed Susan (*Rudbeckia fulgida* 'Gold-sturm'), coneflower (*Echinacea purpurea*) or golden rod (*Solidago*).

Spodiopogon sibiricus

Stipa calamagrostis (syn. *Achnatherum calamagrostis* syn. *Agrostis calamagrostis*)

VALUABLE, LONG-LASTING FEATHER GRASS

❀ 6–9 ○

↕ 60/90 (24/36)

Habit: dense clumps of arching stems.

Leaves: grey-green, narrow lineal, gently arching.

Flowers: appear in June as brush-like, silvery-white

panicles that turn to a camel-hair colour in the autumn.

Position: open, moderately dry to moderately damp soils rich in lime; sunny and warm; short-lived with floppy growth if planted in heavy soils.

Use: in groups in steppe gardens or wildflower gardens or on sunny terraces.

Stipa calamagrostis

Treatment: cut back in spring.

Tried-and-tested varieties:

• **'Lemperg':** similar to species but generally more compact; very attractive flowers; dark-red autumn colouring; 50/70 cm (20/28 in).

• **'Allgäu':** stiffly upright with gently arching panicles; 70/90 cm (28/36 in).

Stipa capillata

Stipa capillata

ORNAMENTAL FEATHER GRASS FOR DRY POSITIONS

❀ 7–9 ○

↑ 40/90 (16/36)

Habit: dense clumps with flower spikes high above them.

Leaves: blue-green, narrow, curled, stiffly upright.

Flowers: upright panicles with thread-like awns (bristles) some 10–20 cm (4–8 in) long; silky sheen; elegantly arching; play attractively in the wind.

The genus *Stipa* (feather grass) includes many interesting species that are highly suitable for a steppe garden. The right location is vital for these plants, which need a sunny position and an open, moderately dry soil that is poor in nutrients. If your garden soils are too rich, they will need to be impoverished with lots of sand or grit.

Stipa gigantea *(golden oats)*

Position: open, dry to moderately dry soils poor in nutrients and rich in lime; full sun; likes warmth; avoid heavy, nutrient-rich soils, which make the leaves rot and shorten the plant's life.

Treatment: self-seeds; remove seedlings if necessary.

Use: singly or in groups in wild-flower gardens, steppe gardens, rock gardens or gravel beds.

Golden oats
Stipa gigantea

FEATHER GRASS WITH AN IMPRESSIVE HABIT

❀ 6–9 ○

↕ 50/200–250 (20/80–100)

Habit: dense clumps of leaves dominated by towering flower stems.

Leaves: blue-green, narrow lineal, evergreen.

Flowers: loose panicles up to 50 cm (20 in) long on stiffly upright stems.

Position: open, dry to moderately dry soils poor in nutrients; sunny and warm; short-lived on damp, nutrient-rich soils.

Treatment: winter protection recommended.

Use: steppe gardens, gravel beds, together with silvery-leaved herbaceous perennials that tolerate dryness.

Stipa pulcherrima nudicostata (often sold as *S. barbata*)

FEATHER GRASS WITH STRIKING SEED HEADS

❀ 7–9 ○

↕ 40/120 (16/48)

Habit: loose clumps.

Leaves: grey-green, long and narrow, often with curled edges.

Flowers: feathery, silvery-coloured flower heads with awns up to 40 cm (16 in) long; elegantly arching; play attractively in the wind.

Position: dry to moderately dry soils; likes lime and warmth; can grow in full sun; extremely short-lived on damper, nutrient-rich soils.

Treatment: maintains itself by self-seeding; thin out seedlings if necessary; remove wilted flowers.

Use: gravel beds and gardens, rock gardens, wildflower gardens.

The most beautiful annual grasses

The ornamental value of annual grasses is mainly associated with their flowers and seed heads, though a few species have interesting growth habits too. Annuals are very short-lived, dying in the autumn after seeding. This means they need to be resown every year in the spring.

It is very rare for annual grasses to be grown for sale, and you will normally have to resort to seed packets from a garden centre. But these grasses will more than repay the extra effort of growing them from seed by flowering long and profusely.

The individual grasses considered below vary greatly in their habit, leaves, stems, flowers and colours. But they are similar in terms of their uses and requirements, and in both respects can be dealt with together:

- **Position:** annual grasses like lots of warmth and need a sunny location. They need well-drained soils with plenty of nutrients.

- **Use:** annual grasses are used mainly with summer flowers or to fill gaps in perennial beds. They make interesting displays in combination with

Briza maxima *(greater quaking grass)*

autumn-flowering perennials, and the seed heads are much prized by florists as an accompaniment to cut flowers.

Greater quaking grass
Briza maxima

❀ 6–8 ○

↑ 30–50 (12–20)

Habit: clump-forming.

Leaves: blue-green, upright, narrow lineal.

Flowers: flower stems carry large, heart-shaped spikes that tremble in the wind; greenish at first, later yellowish white.

Propagating annual grasses

Sowing: from late February to March; place the seed tray in a well-lit position and keep it nicely moist.

Pricking out: after about 3–4 weeks, when the first grass stems become visible, place the seedlings in groups of three to five to create clumps.

Potting: after another 3–4 weeks, transfer the young plants to suitable pots.

Planting out: once the late frosts are over, plant these tender annuals out in the garden.

Lesser quaking grass
Briza minor

❀ 7–8 ⬆ 25 (10) ○

Habit: attractive clumps.

Leaves: blue-green, lineal.

Flowers: tiny, cone-like spikes that tremble in the wind; greenish at first, later yellowish white.

Foxtail barley
Hordeum jubatum

❀ 6–9 ⬆ 40–60 (16–24) ○

Habit: dense, upright clumps.

Leaves: fresh green, narrow lineal, gently drooping.

Flowers: elegantly arching spikes with noticeably long

Hordeum jubatum *(foxtail barley)*

awns that poke gracefully out of the leaves; greenish yellow at first, tipped with violet; ripening to bright yellow.

Good companions	
Annual grasses go well with the following summer flowers	
Antirrhinum majus	Snapdragon
Calendula officinalis	Pot marigold
Callistephus chinensis	China aster
Cleome spinosa	Spider flower
Cosmos bipinnatus	
Rudbeckia hirta	Black-eyed Susan
Salvia coccinea	
Salvia farinacea	Mealy sage
Verbena bonariensis	
Verbena rigida	Lilac vervain
Zinnia elegans	

Hare's-tail grass
Lagurus ovatus

❀ 5–8 ⬆ 20–40 (8–16) ○

Habit: dense clumps.

Leaves: fresh green, lanceolate, upright.

Flowers: short, fluffy, egg-shaped spikes borne on thin stems, covered with woolly white bristles shaped rather like hares' tails.

Witch grass
Panicum capillare

❀ 6–7 ⬆ 60–80 (24–32) ○

Habit: clump-forming.

Leaves: fresh green, broad lanceolate, gracefully arching.

Flowers: finely divided panicles of tiny spikelets that float like a veil above the leaves.

African fountain grass
Pennisetum setaceum

❀ 8–10 🔼 70–100 (28–40) ○

Habit: dense clumps dominated by towering flower stems.

Leaves: grey-green, narrow lineal, arching.

Flowers: long, thin, elegantly arching spikes, pink to purple in colour.

Lagurus ovatus (hare's-tail grass)

Pennisetum villosum (feathertop)

Feathertop
Pennisetum villosum

❀ 8–10 🔼 30–60 (12–24) ○

Habit: loose clumps.

Leaves: blue-green, narrow lineal, arching.

Flowers: whitish green, woolly, spiral, on gently curved stems.

Canary grass
Phalaris canariensis

❀ 7–8 🔼 40–70 (16–28) ○

Habit: upright clumps.

Leaves: blue-green, narrow, reed-like, curved at the tips.

Flowers: cone-like spikes on upright stems; greenish white at first, ripening to greenish yellow.

Ruby grass
Rhynchelytrum repens

❀ 7–9 🔼 50–90 (20–36) ○

Habit: loose clumps.

Leaves: grey-green, narrow lineal, upright.

Flowers: scented brownish to purplish-pink spikelets in feathery pyramidal panicles.

European feather grass
Stipa pennata

❀ 5–6 🔼 30–40 (12–16) ○

Habit: clumps, long-lasting in favourable positions.

Leaves: fresh green, narrow lineal.

Flowers: elegantly curved, with long, silvery bristles.

45

The most beautiful bamboos

Muriel bamboo
Fargesia murieliae (syn. *Sinarundinaria murieliae*)

CLUMP-FORMING BAMBOO

⬆ 200–300 (80–120) ◯–◑

Habit: dense clumps of stiffly upright young shoots that arch over as the foliage increases and become umbrella-shaped with age; dense, creeping rootstock; no runners.

Stem: greenish yellow; the thickness of a finger.

Leaves: light green, lanceolate, tapered, 10 cm (4 in) long by 1.5 cm (0.5 in) wide.

Position: open, damp, nutrient-rich soils; tolerates heat;

In recent years, many specimens of *Fargesia murieliae* (Muriel bamboo) came into flower, with the inevitable consequence that they died once the seeds had been formed. In the meantime a new generation of *Fargesia* varieties has been selected from the seedlings that were created. However, these new varieties have yet to be fully tried and tested.

Fargesia murieliae *(Muriel bamboo)*

sensitive to wetness; generally undemanding.

Treatment: feed regularly and water during dry periods; if the clumps become too dense over the years, they can be reduced by thinning in the spring.

Use: *F. murieliae*, like *F. nitida*, is one of the hardiest of all bamboos – a picturesque plant for solitary positions, even in smaller gardens, in the vicinity of water.

Recommended varieties:

- '**Jumbo**': dense clumps; upright, arching, grows fast; 200 cm (80 in) tall.
- '**Simba**': more delicate than the species; weak-growing; 150–200 cm (60–80 in).
- '**Bimbo**': dense bushes; upright, arching; 150–200 cm (60–80 in).

Fountain bamboo
Fargesia nitida (syn. *Sinarundinaria nitida*)

CLUMP-FORMING BAMBOO

⬆ 200–300 (80–120) ◯–◑

Habit: dense clumps; stems initially upright, later arching over to become umbrella-shaped.

Stem: dark green to purplish brown; the thickness of a finger.

Leaves: dark green, lanceolate, with long pointed tips; 6–10 cm (2.5–4 in) long by 1–1.5 cm (0.5 in) wide; stem and leaves more graceful and finely divided than with *F. murieliae.*

Position: open, damp, nutrient-rich soils; sun to half-shade; will not tolerate waterlogging.

Treatment: plenty of water and nutrients in growing season.

Use: one of the hardiest of all bamboo species; good as a solitary, or for hedges or tubs.

Tried-and-tested variety:

• **'Anceps':** stems gently arching; fine-leaved variety; hardy; 200–300 cm (80–120 in).

Golden-groove bamboo
Phyllostachys aureosulcata

PARTICULARLY HARDY BAMBOO

📏 200–300 (80–120) ○–◐

Habit: loose structure; upright stems arch over gently with age; fast-growing; develops runners that spread a long way.

Stem: dark green with yellow stripes; often only a finger's breadth thick; lower portions often reveal a zigzag pattern.

Leaves: dark green, lanceolate; 10 cm (4 in) long by 1 cm (0.5 in) wide.

Position: damp but well-drained, nutrient-rich soils; sun

to half-shade; a highly adaptable species.

Treatment: needs plenty of water and nutrients during the growing season.

Use: an extremely valuable bamboo that is one of the most reliably hardy of the *Phyllostachys* species; recommended even for situations that would normally be unfavourable; as a solitary in gardens and parks, for bamboo walks, windbreaks or near water.

Phyllostachys aureosulcata

Summary of bamboos	
Giant bamboos (over 5 m/16 ft)	
Phyllostachys viridiglaucescens	
Phyllostachys vivax f. *aureocaulis*	
Tall bamboos (over 3 m/10 ft)	
Phyllostachys aureosulcata	Golden-groove bamboo
Phyllostachys bissetii	
Phyllostachys nigra	Black bamboo
Medium-sized bamboos (over 1.5 m/5 ft)	
Fargesia murieliae	Muriel bamboo
Fargesia nitida	Fountain bamboo
Phyllostachys humilis	
Pseudosasa japonica	Arrow bamboo
Sasa palmata	
Low-growing bamboos (less than 1 m/40 in)	
Pleioblastus humilis f. *pumilus*	
Sasa veitchii	Veitch's bamboo

Tried-and-tested forms:

- *P. a. f. spectabilis*: really beautiful stems, bright yellow with green stripes; highly ornamental and very hardy; solitary; 300–500 cm (120–200 in).

- *P. a. f. aureocaulis*: gorgeous bright golden-yellow stems; very hardy; 300–500 cm (120–200 in).

Phyllostachys nigra *(black bamboo)*

Phyllostachys bissetii

STRONG BAMBOO

⬆ 300–400 (120–160) ◯–◖

Habit: dense, upright stems; grows vigorously; lots of runners and shoots.

Stem: shiny olive-green; slightly arching at the tip.

Leaves: fresh green, lanceolate, 7–12 cm (2.5–5 in) long by 1 cm (0.5 in) wide; dense foliage.

Position: damp but well-drained, nutrient-rich soils; sun to light shade; likes warmth.

Treatment: needs plenty of water and nutrients during growing season; bamboo walks can be kept more elegant and attractive by regular thinning.

Use: especially strong and hardy; only for larger gardens;

grows quickly to form thickets or hedges; rhizome barrier recommended (see page 85).

Phyllostachys humilis

BAMBOO THAT TOLERATES PRUNING

⬆ 300–400 (120–160) ◯–◖

Habit: compact and thicket-like; finely divided; vigorous runner development.

Stem: green, often only the breadth of a finger, stiffly upright.

Leaves: fresh green; small, 8 cm (3 in) long by 1 cm (0.5 in) wide; thick foliage.

Position: open, damp, nutrient-rich soils; sun to light shade; very adaptable.

Treatment: extremely tolerant of pruning; used for bonsai in Japan.

Use: very hardy and robust; always use a rhizome barrier to prevent runners; as a solitary, windbreak or screen, or in tubs; makes a dense hedge if trimmed to 2 m (80 in) in height.

Black bamboo
Phyllostachys nigra

DECORATIVE BAMBOO WITH UNUSUAL STEMS

⬆ 300–600 (120–240) ◯–◖

Habit: loosely upright; outer stems elegantly arching; not many runners; mainly clump-forming in temperate latitudes.

Stem: one-year-old stems green; with time they become

increasingly spotted with dark purple, and eventually turn shiny black all over; 2–3 cm (about 1 in) thick.

Leaves: shiny, dark green, lanceolate; 5–12 cm (2–5 in) long by 1 cm (0.5 in) wide; dense foliage.

Position: deep layers of open, damp, nutrient-rich loam; sun to light shade; moderately hardy.

Treatment: needs plenty of water and nutrients during growing period; some winter protection required; regular thinning, removing older, thinner stems, and straightening the leaning stems around the edges, provides the best view of the mature black stems.

Use: an extremely valuable bamboo on account of its unusual stems; as a solitary, or even in small gardens or atrium gardens.

Tried-and-tested varieties:

• **'Boryana':** green stems, spotted brown with age; robust, vigorously growing variety; develops runners; hardier than species; 500–800 cm (200–320 in).

• *P. n. f. henonis:* young stems light green, later

turning dark green but with no spots; strong, hardy variety; very few runners; 300–600 cm (120–240 in).

Phyllostachys viridiglaucescens

BAMBOO WITH IMPRESSIVE STEMS

↑ 400–900 (160–360) ◑

Habit: stiffly upright at first, becoming elegantly curved; very fast-growing (up to 50 cm/20 in a day on warm days); spreads by means of runners to form an impressive thicket over time; the tallest bamboo that can be grown in temperate climates.

Stem: young stems shiny, fresh green; older stems turn yellowish green; thickness 2–5 cm (1–2 in).

Leaves: shiny, fresh green, lanceolate, 10–15 cm (4–6 in) long by 1–1.5 cm (about 0.5 in) wide.

Position: deep, moist loams with plenty of nutrients; half-shade to light shade; avoid southerly aspects to pre-empt problems with winter sun.

Phyllostachys viridiglaucescens

Don't underestimate the spreading power of bamboos that form runners, such as the majority of *Phyllostachys* species. The best way to contain them is to install a rhizome barrier when you plant them (see page 85) so that their spread is already limited from the outset.

Treatment: install a rhizome barrier to keep runners in check; provide plenty of water and nutrients during the growing season.

Use: a very fast-growing, fast-spreading bamboo, only suitable for spacious sites; fairly hardy.

Pleioblastus viridistriatus *(gold-leaved bamboo)*

Phyllostachys vivax f. *aureocaulis*

ATTRACTIVE SOLITARY BAMBOO

⬆ 400–900 (160–360) ◯–◖

Habit: very fast-growing; develops long runners.

Stem: bright yellow with irregular stripes between the nodes; 4–7 cm (1.5–2.5 in) thick.

Leaves: fresh green, elegantly arching, 10–15 cm (4–6 in) long by 1.5–2.5 cm (0.5–1 in) wide.

Position: deep, well-drained, damp, nutrient-rich soil; sun to half-shade; avoid soils that are too heavy so that the stems can harden off properly for winter.

Treatment: plenty of water and nutrients during the growing season; thin out older shoots and raise up the lower stems to reveal the coloured stems in their full glory.

Use: this form is fairly hardy (hardier than the species); a vigorous and highly attractive bamboo for temperate latitudes; use as a solitary.

Pleioblastus argenteo-striatus f. *pumilus* (syn. *P. pumilus*)

GROUND-COVER BAMBOO

⬆ 50–80 (20–32) ◯–◖

Habit: a dwarf bamboo that becomes very dense and spreads vigorously by means of runners.

Stem: thin, grey stems.

Leaves: bluish green, lanceolate, 10 cm (4 in) long by 1–1.5 cm (about 0.5 in) wide.

Position: damp, nutrient-rich soils; sun to half-shade.

Treatment: from spring onwards, the whole area occupied by the plant can be trimmed, using a lawnmower on a suitably high setting, to create a dense carpet of bamboo.

Pseudosasa japonica *(arrow bamboo)*

Use: invasive ground-cover bamboo; as a replacement for a lawn or as underplanting for shrubs; needs rhizome barriers to hold it in check.

Other species:

- *P. pygmaeus* 'Distichus': small, dense, bushy; fan-like leaves, 5–6 cm (2–2.5 in) long; ground-cover bamboo; height 40 cm (16 in).

- *P. variegatus* (syn. *P. fortunei*): small, dense, bushy; leaves lanceolate with white stripes, 10 cm (4 in) long by 1–1.5 cm (about 0.5 in) wide; good for ground cover; height 40 cm (16 in).

- *P. viridistriatus* (syn. *P. auricomus*) – gold-leaved bamboo: dwarf bamboo, 60–120 cm (24–48 in) tall, with yellow-and-green striped leaves (especially in spring) 20 cm (8 in) long by 2–2.5 cm (about 1 in) wide; good for brightening up shrubberies.

Arrow bamboo
Pseudosasa japonica

LARGE-LEAVED BAMBOO

⬆ 200–300 (80–120)   ◑–●

Habit: stiffly upright stems that begin to arch over as they form branching twigs; develops runners without becoming a nuisance.

Stem: thin, green stems.

Leaves: shiny, dark green, broad lanceolate, large, 20–25 cm (8–10 in) long by 3–4 cm (1–1.5 in) wide; in a fan-like arrangement at the tips of the stems.

Position: damp, nutrient-rich soils; half to full shade; very adaptable.

Treatment: install a rhizome barrier to prevent runners from proliferating and invading other plantings.

Use: a highly decorative and fairly hardy bamboo; as a solitary, near water, in rhododendron gardens or shrubberies.

Sasa palmata

EXOTIC BAMBOO WITH PALM-LIKE LEAVES

⬆ 100–150 (40–60)   ○–◑

Habit: loose structure, slow-growing; develops short

Sasa veitchii (Veitch's bamboo)

If bamboos are damaged in the winter, it's a good idea to wait a while. Often only the leaves die off and the stems regenerate. It's rare for the stems themselves to die so that they have to be removed.

runners that eventually create an impenetrable thicket.

Stem: thin, green, upright.

Leaves: dark green, extremely large, measuring 20–30 cm (8–12 in) long by 5–8 cm (2–3 in) wide; leathery with a noticeable midrib.

Position: damp, nutrient-rich soils; sun to half-shade; thrives in cool, humid conditions.

Treatment: install a rhizome barrier to prevent runners from

Sasa palmata

spreading; moderately hardy, but needs protection from winter sun.

Use: for extensive plantings around ponds or running water, or beneath shrubs; avoid confined spaces.

Veitch's bamboo
Sasa veitchii

BAMBOO WITH DECORATIVE FOLIAGE

⬆ 30–80 (12–32) ◯–◐

Habit: bushy, upright; spreads rapidly by means of vigorous runners; good opportunities for bamboo carpets or even meadows.

Stem: thin, purplish green, very elastic, finely branching.

Leaves: shiny, dark green, large, 25–30 cm (10–12 in) long by 5–8 cm (2–3 in) wide; edges turn increasingly white and parchment-like in the autumn, and remain like this through the winter.

Position: damp, nutrient-rich soils; sun to half-shade; prefers cool, humid situations.

Treatment: rhizome barrier required to keep runners in check; cut back drastically in spring; moderately hardy.

Use: tolerant of tree roots; good underplanting for shrubs, but not for a small area.

The most beautiful ferns

Northern maidenhair fern
Adiantum pedatum

ELEGANT FERN WITH ATTRACTIVE FRONDS

⬆ 40–60 (16–24) ◗–●

Habit: creeps slowly but continuously to form large clumps.

Leaves: fresh-green, spreading, hand-shaped fronds reminiscent of peacocks' tails, borne on wiry, shiny black stems, and sprouting in early April in the form of delicate reddish spirals; bright-yellow autumn colouring.

Position: open, damp, humus-rich soils; light to half-shade; prefers cool, humid situations.

Treatment: plant in shallow soil and leave to grow undisturbed.

Use: decorative fern for light shade on the north side of walls.

Tried-and-tested varieties:

- **'Imbricatum'** (syn. *A. aleuticum* 'Imbricatum'): a dwarf fern with slightly wavy fronds; 20 cm (8 in).

- **'Japonicum'** (syn. *A. aleuticum* 'Japonicum'): new shoots a deep reddish colour, turning gradually green over summer.

Summary of ferns

Large ferns (over 100 cm/40 in)

Athyrium filix-femina	Lady fern
Dryopteris affinis	
Dryopteris dilatata	Broad buckler fern
Dryopteris filix-mas	Male fern
Matteuccia struthiopteris	Ostrich fern
Osmunda regalis	Royal fern

Medium-sized ferns (over 50 cm/20 in)

Adiantum pedatum	Northern maidenhair fern
Athyrium nipponicum 'Metallicum'	Painted fern
Dryopteris erythrosora	Japanese shield fern
Onoclea sensibilis	Sensitive fern
Polystichum aculeatum	Hard shield fern
Polystichum setiferum	Soft shield fern
Thelypteris palustris	Marsh fern

Low-growing ferns (less than 50 cm/20 in)

Adiantum venustum	Kashmir maidenhair fern
Asplenium scolopendrium	Hart's-tongue fern
Asplenium trichomanes	Maidenhair spleenwort
Blechnum spicant	Hard fern
Polypodium vulgare	Common polypody

Adiantum pedatum 'Imbricatum' (syn. A. aleuticum 'Imbricatum')

53

Asplenium scolopendrium 'Crispum'

Kashmir maidenhair fern
Adiantum venustum

DELICATE FERN FOR SHADY GARDENS

⬆ 20–30 (8–12) ◐-●

Habit: long, creeping rhizomes out of which the fronds develop.

Leaves: fresh-green, finely divided, elegantly arching fronds borne on wiry, shiny black stems; bronze autumn colouring.

Now that ferns have become fashionable garden plants again, it means that most good garden centres now offer a wide range of hardy species and varieties.

Position: open, damp soils with plenty of humus and lime; light to full shade.

Treatment: plant in shallow soil; winter protection recommended during first year of planting; sufficiently hardy by the second winter.

Use: in the shelter of rocks and tree stumps, and in rhododendron gardens; combines well with uncompetitive shade perennials.

Hart's tongue fern
Asplenium scolopendrium

ORNAMENTAL EVERGREEN FERN

⬆ 40–50 (16–20) ◐-●

Habit: shuttlecock-shaped clumps.

Leaves: shiny, dark green, elongated lanceolate, tongue-like, leathery, undivided, evergreen.

Position: open, damp soils rich in humus and lime; half to full shade; humid situations.

Treatment: protect from winter sun.

Use: in small groups in shade plantings, in shady rock gardens or along the front of north-facing walls.

Tried-and-tested varieties:

- **'Angustatum'**: very narrow fronds, 40 cm (16 in) long.

- **'Crispum'**: fronds with wavy edges, 30–45 cm (12–18 in) long.

- **'Undulatum'**: fronds less wavy than 'Crispum' but darker green; 30 cm (12 in) long.

Maidenhair spleenwort
Asplenium trichomanes

MINIATURE EVERGREEN FERN

⬆ 15–25 (6–10) ◐

Habit: short, creeping rhizomes; lawn-like under favourable conditions.

Leaves: matt dark-green, almost lineal fronds, made up of opposing ovate leaflets on red-brown to dark-brown stems; evergreen.

Position: open, damp, humus-rich, acid to slightly alkaline soils; half-shade; likes warmth.

Treatment: if planted in gaps in walls, roots must be deeply embedded and well pressed in; rather delicate during the growing phase.

Use: delicate fern for planting in damp shade in cracks in walls and between rocks, next to tree stumps and in shaded rock gardens or miniature gardens.

Lady fern
Athyrium filix-femina

UNDEMANDING FERN FOR WOODLAND GARDENS

↑ 100–150 (40–60) ●

Habit: shuttlecock-shaped clumps, developing over the years by means of short rhizomes to produce wide-spreading, many-headed plants.

Leaves: light-green, gently arching fronds up to 1 m (40 in) high, doubly or triply divided into pointed sections; straw-yellow autumn colouring.

Position: open, damp, heavy, acid, humus-rich loams; shade, though full sun possible if soil is wet; adaptable.

Treatment: water during long periods of dryness.

Use: wildflower gardens, shade plantings in combination with vigorous-growing shrubs.

Tried-and-tested varieties:

- **'Cristatum':** tips of fronds slightly forked; 50–70 cm (20–28 in).

- **'Minutissimum':** miniature lady fern, much weaker-growing than species; 40 cm (16 in).
- **'Plumosum':** more finely divided than species; 60 cm (24 in).
- **'Rotstiel':** like the species except for reddish stems; 100–150 cm (40–60 in).

Painted fern
Athyrium nipponicum var. *pictum*

ORNAMENTAL FERN WITH A METALLIC SHEEN

↑ 50–70 (20–28) ◑

Habit: creeping rootstock; many-headed plant; bushy arrangement of fronds; becomes lawn-like over a number of years.

Leaves: metallic grey-green with reddish-purple ribs and veins, late-sprouting, shrinking in winter; long-stemmed fronds, doubly divided, pointed.

Position: damp, humus-rich, slightly acid soils; light to half-shade; prefers cool, humid situations.

Treatment: light winter protection recommended.

Athyrium filix-femina *(lady fern)*

Use: a jewel among the open-air ferns, creating delightful colour contrasts; combines well with rhododendrons, shrubs and shade-loving grasses.

Athyrium nipponicum *var.* pictum
(painted fern)

Blechnum spicant *(hard fern)*

Hard fern
Blechnum spicant

ATTRACTIVE NATIVE FERN

🌱 20–40 (8–16)   ◖–●

Habit: clump-forming with short rhizomes.

Leaves: shiny, dark-green, leathery, simply divided fronds, forming a rosette on the ground; evergreen.

Position: damp, acid, humus-rich soils; half to full shade; needs moist soil and humid air.

Treatment: difficult plant to establish, being delicate in the first few years; protect from winter sun.

Use: not a very vigorous plant, and liable to be swamped by stronger-growing neighbours, so should only be used in combination with weaker-growing shrubs and grasses; shady gardens.

Dryopteris affinis

IMPRESSIVE YET UNDEMANDING FERN

🌱 100–120 (40–48)   ◖–●

Habit: develops into broad, umbrella-shaped rosettes.

Leaves: fronds dark green with a dull sheen and doubly divided; stems scaly, especially during the sprouting phase; evergreen.

Position: damp, nutrient-rich soils; half to full shade; light shade too if soil is moist enough.

Treatment: very undemanding and easy to look after.

Use: particularly effective in the spring as the young fronds unfurl with their covering of golden-brown scales; an impressive, long-lived fern for shady places.

Broad buckler fern
Dryopteris dilatata

NATIVE FERN WITH ATTRACTIVE FROND CROWNS

🌱 90–150 (36–60)   ●

Habit: large, shuttlecock-shaped clumps.

Leaves: dark-green, arching fronds, triply divided, up to 1 m (40 in) long; evergreen.

Position: open, humus-rich soils poor in lime, in shady locations.

Treatment: large fronds easily broken, so choose a sheltered location.

Use: singly or in small groups, as underplanting for trees and shrubs, or planted over larger areas in woodland gardens.

Dryopteris dilatata *(broad buckler fern)*

Dryopteris erythrosora *(Japanese shield fern)*

Japanese shield fern
Dryopteris erythrosora

PRETTY FERN FOR SHADY GARDENS

↕ 50–75 (20–30) ◑–●

Habit: bushy, developing over the years into a many-headed thicket.

Leaves: shiny dark-green fronds, doubly divided, late-sprouting; young shoots bronze-coloured; young fronds with a reddish tinge; evergreen.

Position: deep, open, humus-rich soils; half to full shade; sunny too if soil is moist enough.

Treatment: don't remove fallen leaves from neighbouring shrubs, as these provide the best winter protection; protect from winter sun; when new shoots sprout, remove old fronds to reveal spring growth in all its beauty.

Use: rhododendron gardens, shade plantings.

Tried-and-tested variety:

• 'Gracilis': more delicate than species; 50 cm (20 in).

Male fern
Dryopteris filix-mas

STRONG BUT ATTRACTIVE WOODLAND FERN

↕ 90–150 (36–60) ◑–●

Habit: upright, umbrella-like clumps.

Leaves: dark-green, gently arching fronds, doubly divided, late-sprouting with beautiful brown shoots.

Position: damp, humus-rich soils; half to full shade; will tolerate sun if soil is moist enough.

Treatment: don't remove any fallen leaves or dead fronds as these will later provide vital nutrients; spray during dry periods.

Use: undemanding woodland fern for wildflower gardens and shade plantings.

Tried-and-tested varieties:

• 'Crispa': like species except for crowded, wavy fronds; 40–50 cm (16–20 in)

• 'Linearis': finely divided fronds; vigorous but not invasive; 70–90 cm (28–36 in).

Where ferns are concerned, it's important not to remove the dead leaves from neighbouring trees and shrubs, as these are essential in providing nutrients. Old fronds should similarly be left throughout the winter, as they will provide natural winter protection, especially for the young shoots.

Matteuccia struthiopteris *(ostrich fern)*

Onoclea sensibilis *(sensitive fern)*

Ostrich fern, shuttlecock fern
Matteuccia struthiopteris

VIGOROUS NATIVE FERN

⬆ 60–120 (24–48) ◐–●

Habit: shuttlecock-shaped clumps, spreading vigorously over time to cover large areas.

Leaves: fresh green, doubly divided, fading with the first frosts of autumn; spore-bearing fronds appear from July to August, first olive-green, later dark brown; very attractive in winter and good as a dried plant.

Position: damp, humus-rich soils in cool, humid situations; half to full shade; full sun also possible if ground is moist enough.

Treatment: check for proliferation; spray during dry periods to prevent fronds turning yellow.

Use: tolerates tree roots; a vigorous, undemanding fern that is likely to become invasive; only suitable for extensive shade plantings.

Similar species:

• *M. pennsylvanica*: can easily be confused with *M. struthiopteris*, but the fronds are lighter green, narrower and more elegant; less invasive than *M. struthiopteris* and also requires less moisture; grows up to 150 cm (60 in) tall.

Sensitive fern
Onoclea sensibilis

VIGOROUS FERN FOR LARGE GARDENS

⬆ 70–90 (28–36) ◐

Habit: spreads by means of creeping rhizomes to cover wide areas.

Leaves: light green, doubly divided and borne on long stems; late-sprouting; develops yellowish-red autumn colouring; short spore-bearing fronds appear in summer with sori that are reminiscent of pearl necklaces.

Position: damp, humus-rich loams; light to half-shade.

Treatment: protect early shoots from frost.

Use: only suitable for large gardens as this fern occupies large areas; the more moisture there is available, the more it will proliferate; a good plant for securing marshy areas or riverbanks.

Tried-and-tested variety:

• **'Rotstiel':** reddish stems; rather smaller and less invasive than the species; 70–80 cm (28–32 in).

Royal fern
Osmunda regalis

ONE OF THE LARGEST NATIVE FERNS

↑ 120–150 (48–60) ●

Habit: upright, forming loose clumps.

Leaves: fresh green, leathery, doubly divided; candle-like spore-bearing fronds; golden-yellow autumn colouring.

Position: damp, acid, humus-rich soils; prefers humid, sheltered, shaded positions; tolerates sun if soil is very moist.

Treatment: avoid transplanting as this will knock back its development.

Use: singly or in loose groups, between or in front of shrubs, or alongside streams and ponds.

Tried-and-tested varieties:

• **'Cristata':** tips of fronds become noticeably forked; no distinctive autumn colouring; 80 cm (28 in).

Osmunda regalis *(royal fern)*

• **'Gracilis':** smaller and more delicate than the species, with red frond stems; 80 cm (28 in).

• **'Purpurascens':** sprouting frond stems purplish red; 80–130 cm (32–52 cm).

Common polypody
Polypodium vulgaris

VALUABLE GROUND-COVER FERN

↑ 20–30 (8–12) ◑-●

Habit: spreads over time by means of creeping rhizomes to form broad carpets of vegetation.

Leaves: dark green, rough, leathery, simply divided, evergreen.

Position: open, lime-free, humus-rich loams; half to full shade; very adaptable.

> Ferns generally prefer open soils with plenty of humus above a well-drained subsoil. You can improve the humus levels by adding some leaf compost and working it thoroughly into the soil.

Polypodium vulgare *(common polypody)*

Most wild ferns live in woodlands, where they are used to fairly constant conditions of damp soil and humid air. This means that during periods of dryness they benefit from regular or even constant spraying to increase the humidity levels.

Treatment: straighforward to look after, and once it has become established it is tolerant of dryness.

Use: in shady areas, or in cracks in rocks or walls.

Hard shield fern
Polystichum aculeatum

HIGHLY ATTRACTIVE EVERGREEN FERN

⬆ 60–80 (24–32) ◐–●

Habit: broad, umbrella-shaped clumps.

Leaves: shiny, dark green, leathery, doubly or triply divided, elegantly arching fronds, evergreen.

Position: open soils with plenty of humus and nutrients; half to full shade.

Treatment: the evergreen fronds remain until the new growth begins in May, so don't cut back until late April or even early May.

Use: singly or in smallish groups; valuable fern for shady gardens, together with rhododendrons, woodland perennials and shade-loving grasses, or for shady rock gardens or in front of walls.

Soft shield fern
Polystichum setiferum

DECORATIVE FERN WITH MANY VARIETIES

⬆ 60–80 (24–32) ◐–●

Habit: broad, umbrella-shaped clumps of loosely arching fronds with a diameter of up to 120 cm (48 in).

Leaves: matt green, finely divided; frond stems covered with a dense layer of scales; evergreen

Position: damp soils with plenty of humus and nutrients; half to full shade; plenty of humidity.

Treatment: to remain evergreen, needs protection from strong winds and winter sun.

Use: singly or in small groups; decorative fern for planting around shrubs, in rhododendron gardens or beneath light-hungry foliage plants.

Tried-and-tested varieties:

- **'Herrenhausen':** broad fronds up to 40 cm (16 in) long; 70 cm (28 in).

- **'Plumosum Densum':** fronds very finely divided, almost moss-like and measuring up to 50 cm (20 in) long; 40 cm (16 in).

• **'Proliferum':** narrow, slightly arching fronds up to 60 cm (24 in) long, developing hosts of tiny plantlets along their midribs; 50 cm (20 in).

Marsh fern
Thelypteris palustris

FINELY DIVIDED FERN FOR DAMP POSITIONS

↑ 60–80 (24–32) ◐-●

Habit: upright fronds that stand singly; spreads by means of runners.

Leaves: fresh green, delicate, doubly divided, elongated lanceolate, 5–15 cm (2–6 in) long; fertile fronds taller but more delicate than sterile fronds.

Position: damp or wet soils, including bogs, ponds or river margins in up to 20 cm (8 in) of water; only tolerates sunlight if there is sufficient water available.

Treatment: plant in containers if there is a danger of its becoming invasive.

Thelypteris palustris *(marsh fern)*

Polystichum setiferum *'Proliferum' produces lots of tiny plantlets.*

Use: this is the only fern that will grow in shallow water, which means it can provide green cover for river margins or shallow ponds, where the finely divided fronds create strong contrasts with neighbouring marsh and water plants.

Ferns, like grasses, can be propagated by means of division, although this is not a very productive method. Spore propagation is much more productive (see page 91), so this is the method preferred by specialist growers and enthusiastic amateurs.

Choosing and combining grasses and ferns

Grasses and ferns are prized mainly for their growth patterns and decorative leaves. Their characteristics can be best appreciated if they are grown in combination with perennials and shrubs, and used skilfully they can bring beauty to any perennial bed.

Location factors

As with all garden plants, the first important thing to consider when using grasses is the right place to plant them, which is essential if they are to thrive. But there are so many different kinds of grasses from so many different habitats in the wild that you will be sure to find a suitable grass for any position in your garden.

The previous chapter gives the location requirements for all the various plants that are described there.

Aesthetic factors

Apart from positional requirements, there are a number of different aesthetic considerations. The main factors to be borne in mind are the shape and colour of the leaves, the growth habit of the plant, and of course the flowers.

Leaf patterns

The elegant lines of grass leaves are among the most highly prized aspects of these plants. They have a highly unified leaf shape that combines very effectively with other shapes and sizes of leaves.

Grass leaves also form interesting contrasts with other leaf patterns such as those formed by finely divided or large-leaved foliage. The more varied the leaf forms, the more exciting the display.

Leaf colours

Quite apart from the size and shape of the leaves, a good variety of colours makes for a fascinating array of designs. Most ornamental grasses are greenish in colour, which means they combine nicely with many other colours. A green background enhances the effect of all the various flower colours.

Deschampsia cespitosa (tufted hair grass) produces a rich display of flower panicles that turn to yellowish-coloured seed heads.

◄ *Grasses can enrich a garden display in all manner of different ways – not least with their glorious autumn colouring.*

When grasses are combined with perennials with contrasting leaf shapes, the results can be quite exciting. Here we have Hakonechloa macra *'Aureola' growing next to* Heuchera *and* Bergenia.

and warmth, making them particularly appropriate for steppe-like plantings.

Grasses with **red- or brown-tinted leaves** are among the

Nowadays there is an amazing range of grass varieties available with attractive white- or yellow-variegated leaves, not to mention the many species and varieties with blue, grey or reddish-coloured leaves.

White- or yellow-variegated grasses work particularly effectively in the darker, more shaded areas of a garden, where they provide a much-needed splash of light. In sunnier positions they make excellent companions for flowering perennials. They look especially elegant in combination with white- or yellow-flowered perennials that imitate the colours of their leaves.

All **blue- and grey-leaved grasses** like plenty of sunshine

Leaf colours

White-variegated grasses for sun to light shade

- *Calamagrostis × acutiflora* 'Overdam'
- *Glyceria maxima* var. *variegata*
- *Miscanthus sinensis* 'Variegatus'
- *Phalaris arundinacea* 'Picta'

for light shade to full shade

- *Carex conica* 'Snowline'
- *Carex* 'Ice Dance'
- *Carex muskingumensis* 'Silberstreif'
- *Carex ornithopoda* 'Variegata'
- *Luzula sylvatica* 'Marginata'
- *Molinia caerulea caerulea* 'Variegata'

Leaf colours

Yellow-variegated grasses for sun to light shade

- *Miscanthus sinensis* 'Strictus' and 'Zebrinus'
- *Phragmites australis* 'Variegatus'
- *Spartina pectinata* 'Aureomarginata'

for light shade to full shade

- *Carex elata* 'Aurea'
- *Carex oshimensis* 'Evergold'
- *Hakonechloa macra* 'Aureola'
- *Luzula sylvatica* 'Wintergold'

Blue grasses for sunny positions

- *Festuca amethystina*
- *Festuca glauca* varieties
- *Festuca ovina* varieties
- *Helictotrichon sempervirens*
- *Koeleria glauca*
- *Stipa gigantea*

Red to red-brown grasses for sunny positions

- *Carex buchananii*
- *Imperata cylindrica* 'Rubra'

more unusual plants. They are most effective when planted in sunny positions with a gradation of other colours. They also make very good pot plants.

Autumn colouring

Many grasses really come into their own in the autumn with a display of flame-red tints. The best autumn colours are achieved by grasses that grow in the sun. Some grasses will admittedly change colour even in light shade, but the resulting tints are generally more subdued. The intensity of colour may also vary depending on the weather, and many grasses retain their colour well into the winter season.

The autumn colours of grasses add an extra dimension to those of deciduous shrubs and autumn-flowering perennials. The panel on the right lists the species and varieties with the best autumn colouring.

Autumn colouring

Grasses with good autumn colours

- *Calamagrostis* × *acutiflora* 'Karl Foerster'
- *Chasmanthium latifolium*
- *Miscanthus* × *giganteus*
- *Miscanthus sinensis* 'Sirene', 'Silver Feather', 'Malepartus'
- *Molinia caerulea caerulea* varieties
- *Molinia caerulea arundinacea* varieties
- *Panicum virgatum* varieties
- *Pennisetum alopecuroides*
- *Schizachyrium scoparium*
- *Spodiopogon sibiricus*

Carex oshimensis *'Evergold' (above) and* Miscanthus sinensis *'Strictus' (below) are two of the most strikingly coloured varieties of grass.*

The intense blue of Festuca glauca *'Elijah Blue' (above) is typical of many varieties of blue fescue.* Carex buchananii *(below) is just as colourful in its own way.*

Perennial beds with grasses reach their zenith in the autumn, when autumn flowers combine with glorious autumn foliage.

Growth habits

As far as ornamental grasses are concerned, the shape and general appearance of a plant is particularly important, because it will remain visible all year round.

The judicious introduction of grasses with particular growth habits can have a dramatic effect on the appearance of a perennial bed. For example, a stiffly upright grass such as *Calamagrostis × acutiflora* 'Karl Foerster' – or a selection of *Miscanthus* varieties – can provide the basic structure for the bed, especially if they are grown in small groups and at regular intervals. On the other hand, the elegantly arching leaves of grasses such as *Pennisetum alopecuroides* can soften up the hard lines of a bed boundary or path edge.

Flowers and seed heads

Many grasses produce an ornate display of flowers that grow much taller than the leaves. Most grasses wait until summer before coming into flower. There then follows a delightful interplay of colours as the flowers ripen into seed heads with golden-yellow, coppery or reddish-brown tints.

The flowers and seed heads combine particularly well with autumn-flowering perennials. There are many species and varieties of grass that retain their seed heads well into the winter season. Then there are some grasses whose flowers and seed heads are used in a variety of ways in flower arranging.

The table opposite lists some of the grasses with the most decorative flowers and seed heads.

Winter appearance

Grasses should generally be left until the spring before you cut them back, as they often retain their attractiveness throughout the winter. Besides which, the dried-up leaves provide natural protection from the cold. A covering of snow or hoar frost can turn their brownish autumn tints into a veritable winter wonderland. And provided the autumn hasn't been too damp, the leaves will retain their shape throughout the winter. In this way they help to fill the bare spaces that often appear during the cold season.

There are some varieties of *Miscanthus* that have proved particularly strong and sturdy, keeping their shape beneath the weight of snow. And a winter garden can be very much enriched by the presence of certain evergreen grasses such

Three dramatic-looking grasses – the stiffly upright Calamagrostis × acutiflora *'Karl Foerster' (left) contrasts nicely with the elegant leaves of* Pennisetum alopecuroides *(centre) and the porcupine-like habit of* Helictotrichon sempervirens *(right).*

Grasses with striking flowers or seed heads

- *Bouteloua gracilis*
- *Briza media*
- *Calamagrostis brachytricha*
- *Carex grayi*
- *Carex pseudocyperus*
- *Chasmanthium latifolium*
- *Eriophorum latifolium*
- *Hystrix patula*
- *Luzula nivea*
- *Melica cicilata*
- *Miscanthus sinensis* 'Silver Feather' and 'Silberspinne'
- *Molinia caerulea arundinacea*
- *Panicum virgatum* varieties
- *Pennisetum alopecuroides*
- *Stipa calamagrostis*
- *Stipa capillata*
- *Stipa gigantea*
- *Stipa pulcherrima nudicostata*

Two plants with attractive seed heads – Pennisetum alopecuroides *(Chinese fountain grass, left) and* Chasmanthium latifolium *(spangle grass, right).*

Leave your grasses intact until the spring, and you will be rewarded with some glorious winter vistas, where snow and hoar frost make for magical effects.

as *Carex morrowii* 'Variegata', *Carex plantaginea* or *Luzula sylvatica*.

Spatial factors

Grasses generally work best when planted **singly** or in **small groups**. They may, for example, be planted at regular or irregular intervals to provide structure in perennial beds. Among the most suitable grasses for adding structure to a bed are *Calamagrostis* × *acutiflora* 'Karl Foerster', *Panicum virgatum* (switch grass) and numerous varieties of *Miscanthus*.

A few grasses can be used to fill **small areas**. These include

Carex plantaginea and *Luzula sylvatica*.

Some grasses grow into remarkably large plants, whose true beauty can only be fully appreciated if they are grown as **specimens** or **solitaries**. Examples of this include *Miscanthus* × *giganteus* and many varieties of *Miscanthus sinensis* (eulalia grass). As solitaries they are particularly effective if they are planted near a resting point in a garden such as a path, a patio, a pond or a seat, or perhaps even in a courtyard.

The panel above right gives the recommended space that should be allowed for grasses of different sizes.

Large, impressive grasses such as Stipa gigantea (golden oats) are best seen in solitary splendour.

Planting opportunities

Grasses for sunny perennial beds

There is a wide choice of grasses available for sunny situations. Like all sun-loving perennials, these grasses thrive best on well-drained soils in the full sun.

Depending on their size, such grasses may be used as background or structure plants, or as green companion plants. Low-growing or medium-sized grasses are good for hiding the tall, bare stems of taller perennials. As green companion

Clumps of Molinia caerulea arundinacea *'Windspiel' provide a highly effective framework for various autumn-flowering perennials such as* Aster novi-belgii *(Michaelmas daisy).*

Grasses for sunny situations

- *Calamagrostis* × *acutiflora*
- *Calamagrostis brachytricha*
- *Miscanthus* × *giganteus*
- *Miscanthus sinensis* varieties
- *Molinia caerulea arundinacea* varieties
- *Panicum virgatum* varieties
- *Pennisetum alopecuroides*
- *Schizachyrium scoparium*
- *Sorghastrum nutans*
- *Spodiopogon sibiricus*
- *Sporobolus heterolepis* 'Wisconsin Strain'

plants they create a restful foil for the strong colours of sun-loving perennials.

All the grasses listed in the panel on the left combine well with summer-flowering perennials such as *Phlox paniculata*, *Heliopsis helianthoides* or *Rudbeckia fulgida* (black-eyed Susan). They also go well with the various autumn-flowering Michaelmas daisies such as *Aster novi-belgii*, *A. dumosus* or *A. novae-angliae*.

Grasses for steppe gardens

Certain grasses are an indispensable part of steppe gardens or steppe-like plantings. Steppe grasses need a sunny position with soil that is well-drained and not too rich in nutrients.

As might be imagined, they are generally tolerant of summer drought. Steppe grasses therefore combine best with perennials and sub-shrubs that are similarly tolerant of drought. Suitable examples of these might include bearded iris (*Iris* Barbata hybrids), various species of sage (*Salvia officinalis*, *S. nemorosa* etc.), *Euphorbia seguieriana* and many other grey-leaved perennials.

Grasses for containers

- *Carex oshimensis* 'Evergold'
- *Carex × digitata*
- *Festuca glauca*
- *Festuca ovina*
- *Glyceria maxima* var. *variegata*
- *Hakonechloa macra* 'Aureola'
- *Imperata cylindrica* 'Rubra'
- *Miscanthus sinensis* varieties
- *Phalaris arundinacea* 'Picta'
- *Phragmites australis* 'Variegatus'

Grasses combine with flowering perennials to create a varied display that is further enhanced by the interplay of different colours, shapes and growth patterns.

Grasses for steppe gardens

- *Bouteloua oligostachya*
- *Briza media*
- *Carex montana*
- *Cortaderia selloana*
- *Festuca amethystina*
- *Festuca gautieri*
- *Festuca glauca*
- *Festuca mairei*
- *Festuca ovina*
- *Helictotrichon sempervirens*
- *Hystrix patula*
- *Koeleria glauca*
- *Melica ciliata*
- *Sesleria autumnalis*
- *Stipa calamagrostis*
- *Stipa capillata*
- *Stipa gigantea*
- *Stipa pulcherrima nudicostata*

A harmoniously planted perennial bed in which yellow, purple and white flower colours predominate. The tall, feathery flower heads of golden oats (Stipa gigantea) *punctuate the display.*

Grasses for shady gardens

Shade grasses work very effectively in combination with ferns. See page 76 for some design ideas for shady gardens with grasses and ferns.

Grasses for water gardens or water margins

Grasses often play a dominant role in water gardens and riverbank plantings. The long leaves of ornamental grasses create an excellent foil for the large leaves of many water plants.

When choosing suitable grasses, however, you should take careful note of the required water depths and the fact that some of these grasses can be very invasive. The panel

Grasses for water gardens and water margins

- *Carex grayi*
- *Carex pseudocyperus*
- *Carex muskingumensis*
- *Eriophorum latifolium*
- *Glyceria maxima* var. *variegata*
- *Juncus effusus* 'Spiralis'
- *Phragmites australis*
- *Schoenoplectus lacustris*
- *Spartina pectinata* 'Aureomarginata'

Grasses in tubs can be very effective. Here is a specimen of Hakonechloa macra *'Aureola'.*

below left lists some of the best grasses for watery situations.

Grasses for containers

There are also many grasses that make excellent pot or tub plants. Those with colourful leaves are perhaps the best candidates for this.

Containers are often the best solution for those species and varieties that are not fully hardy, because they can be moved to a suitably protected position as winter approaches. Tubs can also be the best place for growing certain grasses such as *Glyceria maxima* var. *variegata* that might be too invasive if grown out in the garden.

The panel on page 70 (top right) shows other grasses that grow well in containers.

Annual grasses

Annual grasses are essential for beds of summer flowers, where they may provide structure or simply a green background for the many flower colours.

Annual grasses can also be used as space fillers in perennial beds. They are especially suitable if they flower at the same time as the summer-flowering and/or autumn-flowering perennials. Their seed heads are also much sought after by flower arrangers.

The table on page 44 lists some of the most attractive summer flowers that may be successfully combined with annual grasses.

Annual grasses combine very well with summer flowers – in this case Pennisetum villosum *(feathertop) with* Rudbeckia hirta *(black-eyed Susan).*

Using bamboos requires a certain sensitivity – these exotic-looking plants can easily look out of place in a typical English garden.

Bamboos – a touch of the Orient

There are many different ways of incorporating bamboos into a garden design. Their most attractive features include their elegant growth habits, their finely divided evergreen leaves and their beautiful stems.

There are species and varieties available to fulfil every need as regards size, shape or function within the garden. Bamboos can be used as **solitaries**, in **bamboo walks**, as **ground cover**, or as **evergreen hedges** or **screens**. Bamboos are particularly suitable for planting in **courtyards** because of the shelter these places provide. There are many bamboos that can be

planted here that would be insufficiently hardy for planting in more open situations.

Bamboos are especially popular for use with **modern architecture**, because they harmonise so well with materials such as glass, steel and concrete.

In places where it is impossible to plant bamboos out, they will also thrive as **container plants**, provided they receive the necessary extra care. Bamboos in tubs make an attractive addition to any patio, balcony or roof garden.

Companion plants for bamboos

When planting bamboos in your garden, you should always bear

in mind that they have an exotic feel about them, and can look out of place if they are used in the wrong kind of context. The best plants to use with bamboos are naturally those with similarly Asiatic origins.

If you plant them next to large-leaved shrubs and perennials such as *Rodgersia*, *Hosta* or *Mahonia bealei*, the resulting contrasts in shape, and the interplay of different greens, will make for a thoroughly exciting display.

Bamboos as solitaries

Their elegant growth habits and the emphatic lines of their stems make bamboos ideal candidates for use as solitary specimens. A bamboo specimen needs plenty of open space and a neutral background in order to be appreciated at its best.

Good solitary bamboos

- *Phyllostachys aureosulcata*
- *Phyllostachys nigra*
- *Phyllostachys vivax* f. *aureocaulis*
- *Pseudosasa japonica*

Fargesia nitida and *F. murieliae* varieties make good solitaries for smaller gardens.

Bamboos planted next to water are particularly attractive, especially as their colours and shapes are reflected in the water. However, they should not be allowed to stand in the water itself as they are very sensitive to damp, which causes the rhizomes to rot. You will also need to install a rhizome barrier (see page 85) to prevent the rhizomes from penetrating the plastic lining of a pond or watercourse.

A bamboo walk

Some bamboo species and varieties will spread gradually over the years into an impressive group of plants that might eventually form the basis of a bamboo walk.

If you want to create a bamboo walk, you'll need a large garden and plenty of patience, as it won't achieve its full dimensions until some seven to ten years have passed. You'll also need to find a position with a favourable climate.

Depending on the eventual area that you plan to cover, you should start with at least three to five plants, and at the same time you should install a rhizome barrier (see page 85) around the area to be covered.

Regular maintenance should include thinning out to retain the elegance and transparency of the bamboo walk.

The taller-growing *Phyllostachys* species are the most suitable bamboos for the purpose. The following are particularly recommended:

- *P. aureosulcata* (golden-groove bamboo)
- *P. bissetii*
- *P. viridiglaucescens*.

Low-growing bamboos such as Pleioblastus variegatus *are very suitable for use as underplanting for shrubs.*

Companion plants for bamboos	
Shrubs	
Acer palmatum varieties	Japanese maple
Acer japonicum varieties	Japanese maple
Hydrangea aspera	
Ilex crenata	Japanese holly
Prunus laurocerasus	Cherry laurel
Mahonia bealei	
Rhododendron species and varieties	Rhododendron
Viburnum carlesii	
Perennials	
Astilboides tabularis syn. *Rodgersia tabularis*	
Hemerocallis species and varieties	Daylily
Hosta species and varieties	Plantain lily
Kirengeshoma palmata	
Rodgersia species	
Matteuccia struthiopteris	Ostrich fern
Osmunda regalis	Royal fern
Carex morrowii 'Variegata'	
Hakonechloa macra 'Aureola'	
Spartina pectinata 'Aureomarginata'	

Some bamboos can even be grown as hedges, which being evergreen provide excellent screening.

Regular cutting back will keep them lower and denser. In Japan they are often kept so short that they substitute as lawns.

However, you should always bear in mind that these bamboos are by nature invasive. They should never be planted with perennials or small shrubs, which will be unable to compete with them for very long. You should install a rhizome barrier to prevent them spreading beyond the area intended.

Good ground-cover bamboos

- *Pleioblastus argenteostriatus* f. *pumilus*
- *Pleioblastus variegatus*
- *Pleioblastus viridistriatus*
- *Pleioblastus pygmaeus* 'Distichus'
- *Sasa veitchii*

Bamboos as ground cover

Low-growing forms of *Pleioblastus* and *Sasa* spread very fast by means of runners, so are ideal for use as ground-cover. They are also vigorous, evergreen and practically indestructible.

Pleioblastus species form dense carpets within a short period, making them good underplanting for shrubs in light shade or half-shade. It is usually enough to plant one to four plants per square metre/yard, depending on how quickly you want to fill the space. With a density of 1–4 plants/m² (per sq yd) it usually takes between three and four years. With 5–8 plants/m² (per sq yd) the area will be covered in only two years. These species are also very good for stabilising steep slopes or embankments.

All ground-cover bamboos are extremely tolerant of pruning.

A bamboo hedge

Bamboo hedges provide the ideal screen. They have a less formal, more lively appearance than other evergreen hedges.

They only work as informal hedges, because formal pruning goes against their natural growth pattern. If you're using a species that spreads, you'll need to install a rhizome barrier (see page 85) to stop the hedge spreading outwards.

The height and density of the hedge will be determined by whatever species or variety you choose. Depending on what function the hedge is to fulfil, you could choose either a compact species with dense foliage and lots of stems, or a taller, more elegant species with decorative stems.

You can make the hedge denser by thinning out the older, less attractive stems (see page 86). This will encourage the plant to produce new canes.

Good bamboos for hedges

- *Phyllostachys bissetii*
- *Phyllostachys aureosulcata*
- *Fargesia murieliae* 'Bimbo'
- *Fargesia murieliae* 'Jumbo'
- *Fargesia murieliae* 'Simba'

Bamboos in containers

Bamboos in tubs can look extremely attractive, and the fact that they can be moved makes them very adaptable. However, the limited planting space means they require more maintenance than bamboos in the garden.

The following important points should be noted if you want bamboos in tubs to grow properly:

- The container must be big enough – ideally about three times the volume of the root ball. It must be frost-resistant, with a minimum capacity of 50 litres (11 gallons). Drainage holes are needed in the bottom of the tub to prevent the rhizomes from rotting.
- The planting medium should be open and well structured with plenty of nutrients. Regular feeding is required from the second year of planting.
- The most important requirement is regular watering, even on frost-free days in winter.
- It's important to choose the right species or variety. If the tub is to remain outside during the winter, then you need a suitably hardy variety.
- The best way to protect the plant in winter is to sink the tub into the ground. A possible alternative to this might be to insulate it with bubble polythene or straw. Such insulation is needed in order to prevent the root ball from freezing.
- Non-hardy bamboo species should be kept frost-free at a

Good bamboos for tubs

- *Fargesia nitida*
- *Fargesia murieliae* varieties
- *Pseudosasa japonica*
- *Pleioblastus viridistriatus*

temperature of at least 5°C (41°F). Tropical species need at least 10°C (50°F). Because they are evergreen, bamboos need to be kept in a well-lit position. Dark rooms or cellars are totally unsuitable for these plants.

Bamboos can look very good in tubs, though they need lots of watering.

Choosing ferns

Ferns, unlike grasses, are used exclusively as foliage plants. They are particularly interesting for the variety of their leaf patterns and their various shades of green.

Ferns for a shady garden

Most ferns are woodland plants. They therefore need humid air and damp soils with plenty of humus.

These conditions are best found in the light shade that is to be found beneath trees and shrubs. The best plants for providing shade are trees with deep roots and open crowns, which allow enough light to penetrate their leaves to enable the plants beneath them to grow properly. The most suitable trees are Scots pines (*Pinus sylvestris*) and various species of larch (*Larix*). Smaller alternatives might include ornamental fruit trees such as plums (*Prunus*), apples (*Malus*) or *Amelanchier lamarckii* (a species of serviceberry).

Other places where ferns grow well are shaded or half-shaded courtyards and the shade of high walls.

Grasses for a shady garden

- *Carex elata* 'Aurea'
- *Carex morrowii* 'Variegata'
- *Carex ornithopoda* 'Variegata'
- *Carex oshimensis* 'Evergold'
- *Carex pendula*
- *Carex plantaginea*
- *Carex remota*
- *Carex sylvatica*
- *Deschampsia cespitosa*
- *Hakonechloa macra* 'Aureola'
- *Luzula nivea*
- *Luzula sylvatica*
- *Milium effusum* 'Aureum'

The best companions for ferns are shade-loving perennials, including the many shade-loving grasses, some of which are listed in the panel above. The most interesting combination of plants for the shade or half-shade is one that incorporates the greatest variety of leaf sizes, leaf patterns and leaf colours.

There is another group of plants apart from ferns and grasses that is indispensable for shade plantings, and that is large-leaved plants such as *Rodgersia* and *Hosta* (plantain lilies). Their substantial leaves offer the maximum contrast to the leaves and fronds of grasses and ferns.

In shady gardens, the various leaf patterns and the different shades of green come very much to the fore.

The table on the right provides a small selection of the best shade perennials available.

Yet another delightful feature of shady gardens is the interplay of light and shade, which varies continually as the plants move about in the wind, and also changes with the march of the seasons.

Spatial factors

Ferns can be planted singly or in groups depending on their size. Larger species such as royal fern (*Osmunda regalis*) are most effective when planted singly or even as solitaries. Only a very few species are suitable for ground cover over small areas – the Kashmir maidenhair

Flowering plants for a shady garden				
Botanic name	**Common name**	**Flower colour**	**Season**	**Height (cm/in)**
Actaea (syn. Cimicifuga) species		white	7–9	120–150/50–60
Aruncus dioicus	goatsbeard	white	6–7	150–200/60–80
Astrantia major	masterwort	silvery white	6–8	50–70/20–30
Bergenia cordifolia		white, pink	4–5	30–40/1216
Epimedium species		yellow, white, red	4–5	15–25/6–10
Euphorbia amygdaloides	wood spurge	yellowish green	4–5	30–60/12–24
Helleborus species	hellebore, Lenten rose	yellowish green	2–4	25–40/10–16
Hosta species and varieties	plantain lily	white, purple	6–8	10–120/4–50
Kirengeshoma palmata		soft yellow	8–9	60–90/24–36
Polygonatum multiflorum		white	5–6	60–100/24–40
Pulmonaria species and varieties	lungwort	blue, pink, white	3–5	20–30/8–12
Rodgersia species and varieties		creamy white	6–7	80–180/32–70
Tiarella cordifolia	foamflower	creamy white	5–6	15–30/6–12
Vinca minor	lesser periwinkle	light blue, white	4–5	10–20/4–8

Ferns can provide enrichment for any spring garden, especially as their fresh-green fronds begin to unfurl.

fern (*Adiantum venustum*), for example.

The same applies to any accompanying perennials. Plants that develop into larger clumps, such as *Aruncus dioicus* (goatsbeard), should be planted singly, while smaller species such as *Bergenia cordifolia* or *Astrantia major* (masterwort) are most effective when planted in groups of three to five. Low-growing plants such as *Epimedium* species can be planted in larger groups of, say, nine to eleven.

All perennials should be planted with their eventual size in mind, otherwise they will not give of their best. The most effective way to arrange a bed is with taller perennials behind and lower-growing plants in front, and with the medium-sized plants graded in between.

Bulb plants for a spring garden			
Anemone nemorosa	wood anemone	white	3–4
Anemone blanda		blue	3–4
Eranthis hyemalis	winter aconite	yellow	2–3
Galanthus nivalis	common snowdrop	white	2–3
Hyacinthoides hispanica	Spanish bluebell	blue	5
Leucojum vernum	spring snowflake	white	2–3

Ferns and rhododendrons have very similar soil and light requirements, and no rhododendron garden should be without ferns.

A spring garden with ferns

Ferns are particularly attractive during their sprouting phase, not only on account of their fresh-green tints but because of the shapes they create. The tiny unfurling fronds bring new delights every spring.

Perhaps the best ferns in this respect are royal fern (*Osmunda regalis*), lady fern (*Athyrium filix-femina*), ostrich or shuttlecock fern (*Matteuccia struthiopteris*) and hart's-tongue fern (*Asplenium scolopendrium*), not to mention the many and varied forms of buckler fern (*Dryopteris*).

The best spring-flowering companions for ferns include *Lathyrus vernus* (spring-flowering pea), *Brunnera macrophylla*, *Omphalodes verna* (blue-eyed Mary), *Pulmonaria* (lungwort) and *Waldsteinia*, all of which come into flower in May.

Spring-flowering bulbs are yet another essential part of the display. They too come into bloom just as the ferns are beginning to sprout, and when they have finished flowering their dying leaves are conveniently concealed by the developing fronds.

Ferns and grasses in a rhododendron garden

A rhododendron garden provides the ideal growing conditions for ferns and shade-loving grasses, as they have similar soil requirements to rhododendrons. In addition to this, the long leaves of the grasses and the feathery, fresh-green fronds of the ferns provide striking contrasts with the large, leathery, dark-green leaves of the evergreen rhodo-

Shady rock gardens and stone walls provide the ideal conditions for many small, rock-loving ferns.

dendrons. Moreover, the glorious colours of the rhododendron blooms are displayed most powerfully in the company of ferns, grasses and shade-loving perennials.

Ferns for shaded sections of a rock garden

Some ferns, such as those listed on the left are particularly fond of the cracks between rocks. They therefore grow best in the shady sections of a rock garden, or ideally in the damp, shady cracks between the stones of a garden wall that is shaded from the midday sun.

Ferns for shaded sections of a rock garden
Adiantum venustum Kashmir maidenhair fern
Asplenium scolopendrium Hart's-tongue fern
Asplenium trichomanes Maidenhair spleenwort
Blechnum spicant Hard fern
Polypodium vulgare Common polypody

at a glance

- **Grasses** can be found everywhere in the wild, which means there are suitable species for every position in a garden.

- **Bamboos** come in a very wide range of forms suitable for different uses and situations; they can be planted as solitaries, for hedges, for ground cover or even in tubs.

- **Ferns** are used exclusively as foliage plants, and are most at home in the shade of trees and shrubs, or in the cracks in a garden wall.

Planting and maintenance

Provided you plant them in a suitable position, grasses and ferns should last a long time and require relatively little maintenance. However, one or two pointers are worth making with regard to planting and maintenance, if only to ensure continued success.

The best time for planting out grasses is the spring after the ground has begun to warm up.

Planting and maintaining grasses

When to plant

Nowadays, a perennial bed without grasses would be practically inconceivable, and grasses have become very much a standard item in garden centres. The range of grasses on offer has also increased dramatically.

Grasses are cultivated in pots, and can theoretically be planted out at any time of year. But the optimum conditions for planting out grasses are to be found in the spring. The ground has already warmed up a little, so rooting can begin immediately. In the autumn the grass roots are no longer very active; they are reluctant to grow and also liable to rot.

◀ *Grasses are invariably sold in pots, and should be thoroughly watered before they are planted out. Spring is the best time to do this.*

Where to plant

Before planting, make sure you've chosen the right grasses for the right positions. Given the variety of grasses available, this chapter can only give general advice. But the plant descriptions given on page 16 onwards should provide all the information you need.

Preparing the soil

Shade-loving grasses are like ferns in that they need open, humus-rich soils. You can raise the humus levels in the soil by digging in plenty of well-rotted garden compost, leaf compost or peat.

Steppe grasses need open, airy soils with good drainage and not too many nutrients. If the soil is too rich, it can be impoverished by the addition of sand and gravel.

Grasses for perennial beds like damp soils with plenty of humus and loam. The soil

structure can be improved by the addition of well-rotted garden compost.

Feeding

One important task is regular feeding of grasses, taking into account the individual requirements of different plant species

Fertiliser requirements for grasses
Grasses in shade or half-shade 30–40 g/m² (appr. 1 oz/sq yd)
Steppe grasses 40–50 g/m² (1–1.5 oz/sq yd)
Grasses in perennial beds 50–100 g/m² (1.5–3 oz/sq yd) (depending on size)

Grasses can be cut back to ground level, but not until the winter is over.

(see the descriptions on page 16 ff.). Both mineral and organic fertilisers have proved successful. The panel on the previous page gives some general indications.

Cutting back

Grasses should never be drastically cut back until the spring, because the old leaves provide excellent winter protection. Many species are vulnerable to rot if they are cut back in the autumn. Besides which, the grass clumps and the seed heads have a certain decorative value during the winter months, when their beautiful

patterns and shapes may be highlighted by hoar frost and snow.

All deciduous grasses should be cut right back to ground level in the spring. With evergreen grasses, on the other hand, it is usually sufficient to remove damaged leaves, and they only need to be cut back completely if a severe winter has resulted in widespread leaf damage.

Dividing and rejuvenating old grasses

This job is only required after some years have passed. If a grass clump has started to look rather bare in the centre, then it's time for a little rejuvenation. You should divide the clump using a spade, and replant the resulting sections in suitably prepared soil.

Stopping grass from spreading

Some grasses that form runners are very fast-spreading, to the extent that they may easily become invasive. Such species should be watched very carefully for any signs that they may be getting out of hand, and regularly reduced with a spade.

Seedlings

Where grass **varieties** are self-seeding, the seedlings should be removed as the results are generally less attractive than the pure varieties. They may also grow more vigorously, which means that with time they could swamp the original variety. Examples of this include the highly vigorous seedlings of some *Miscanthus* varieties and the seedlings of golden millet (*Milium effusum* 'Aureum'), which revert towards the green leaved form of the species.

With **species** grasses, however seedlings are generally viewed a

If grasses start to look bare in the centre, then it's time for them to be divided and rejuvenated.

Pampas grass (Cortaderia) *can be tied together and surrounded with leaves to protect it from winter damp.*

Nearly all grasses can be easily propagated by division, and the best time for this is the spring.

grasses need no more than a layer of dry leaves secured with brushwood. With pampas grasses (*Cortaderia*) the clumps can be tied up and surrounded with leaves secured with brushwood. The protection should be removed in the spring so that the grasses can be cut back.

Evergreen grasses are best protected at the planting stage by being placed in a position that is protected from winter sun.

Propagation

The majority of grasses are propagated **vegetatively** by means of division. This is done in the spring, and the best time to do this is when the new leaf stems are just beginning to sprout. The process is the same as for rejuvenation (see above), whereby small sections are removed with a spade and immediately replanted in prepared soil.

All **annual grasses** are propagated by **seed**, which should be sown in the spring. The seedlings should be pricked out after three or four weeks, then potted after a further three to four weeks. They can be planted out when the late frosts have finished.

desirable. This is especially true of some feather grasses (*Stipa capillata, S. pulcherrima nudicostata*), which being short-lived depend on self-seeding to survive. The seedlings should only be thinned if they are becoming too crowded.

Winter protection

Some grasses are vulnerable to winter damp and need extra protection if they are in exposed positions. Smaller

Planting and maintaining bamboos

Some bamboo plants can be bought from tree nurseries and garden centres. But the much larger bamboos are sold by specialist gardening outlets that concentrate exclusively on bamboos. Such centres provide hundreds of bamboo species and varieties, which means you should be able to find a suitable bamboo for any position in the garden.

When to plant

The best time to plant bamboos is between March and October. **Spring planting** is the best option in places with a less favourable climate, as it provides the best conditions for establishing plants and ensuring that they continue to thrive.

Clump-forming bamboos spread very slowly, and their stems grow very close together.

Planting in spring means the young plants have plenty of opportunity to put down good roots to enable them to survive the first winter intact. The new roots are essential for these evergreen plants to be able to obtain sufficient water during the winter months.

If you plant bamboos during the summer, you'll need to provide extra water and take great care to ensure that the still fragile young stems aren't broken.

Where to plant

The right position is essential to success, so you should always choose the right species or variety for the particular position in the garden that is to be occupied.

Most bamboos prefer a sheltered position in sun or light shade. Light shade is ideal during the winter as it protects the plants from strong winter sun. Never plant bamboos where they are exposed to wind or strong sunlight, as this can lead to problems with winter frosts (see page 87).

Some low-growing bamboos such as *Pleioblastus* prefer half-shade or even full shade, which makes them suitable for under-planting around trees and shrubs.

Soil requirements

Bamboos like damp but well-drained soils. **Avoid water-logging at all costs**, because these plants are sensitive and react very badly to this.

The ideal soil is a combination of sand, humus and loam with plenty of nutrients. The pH value should ideally be between 5.5 and 6.8 – i.e. neutral to slightly acidic – but this is less important than the other soil requirements.

Bamboos also require lots of watering and plenty of humidity.

Improving the soil

If your soils are heavy and liable to become waterlogged, special preparations are needed to improve the drainage. The best solution is to dig over the soil while adding plenty of sand and gravel.

Planting

The planting hole for a bamboo plant should have at least twice the diameter of the root ball. As bamboos need plenty of humus and nutrients, it's a good idea to add some well-rotted garden compost to the soil you dig up, carefully mixing it in. If you don't have any compost available, then it's sensible to add

Bamboos that develop runners will need plenty of space to spread, though they can be kept in check by means of a rhizome barrier.

some hoof and horn as a base fertiliser, adding between 100 g and 150 g (4–6 oz) depending on the size of the bamboo.

Don't plant bamboos too deep! The top of the root ball should be covered with only a thin layer of soil.

After you've finished planting, tread the soil down well, water thoroughly, and finally add a mulch layer. The best mulching materials are bark humus, garden compost and leaf compost. However, as some of these mulches may deplete the soil of nitrogen as they are broken down by micro-organisms, an extra 50 g/m^2 (1.5 oz/sq yd) of fertiliser may be needed.

Stopping bamboos from spreading

If you want to prevent runner-forming bamboos from getting out of hand at a later stage, then it's important to take preventative measures as early as possible.

The best solution is to install a **rhizome barrier** at the planting stage. The best materials to use for this are rustproof metal strips, concrete rings, corrugated plastic or the plastic rhizome barriers available from specialist outlets or mail-order suppliers.

Pliable materials such as plastic are preferable if you want to create a natural-looking barrier.

The following bamboos form runners and may require a rhizome barrier:
• *Phyllostachys*
• *Pleioblastus*
• *Pseudosasa*
• *Sasa*.

Fargesia species are among the clump-forming bamboos that don't require a rhizome barrier.

Installing a rhizome barrier
A rhizome barrier should be sunk about 70 cm (28 in) into the ground and should protrude some 4–5 cm (1.5–2 in) above the soil. This means that any rhizomes that escape the barrier can be easily removed. The ends of the barrier should overlap well.

The extra effort involved in installing a rhizome barrier at the start is much less than the effort that will otherwise be required in the future to keep the runners in check. Once bamboos start to spread unchecked, the only means of restraint is laborious digging to locate and remove all the offending rhizomes. Installing a barrier is very much the lesser of the two evils.

Bamboos that develop runners can be kept in check by means of a rhizome barrier, which should be installed at the planting stage.

Maintenance tasks

Watering
Bamboos need plenty of water and nutrients during the summer growing season. Both of these are necessary to the formation of the tall, strong canes that are the chief attraction of many species and varieties. This therefore means that continual watering is

> Thin pond-lining materials are not strong enough for use as a rhizome barrier, as they are easily punctured by the sharp tips of bamboo rhizomes.

essential during dry periods. One sure sign of water deprivation is when the leaves start to curl up.

Fertilising

Bamboos have large nutrient requirements. The recommended annual fertiliser dose is 50–150 g/m² (1.5–4.5 oz/sq yd) depending on the size of the particular plant.

The most suitable feeds include high-nitrogen, multi-nutrient mineral fertilisers or organic fertilisers such as hoof and horn. Bamboos are sensitive to salts, so **low-salt fertilisers** are recommended.

Any leaves that fall from bamboos should simply be left, as they are an important source of nutrients.

Mineral fertilisers are quick-acting, so should be given in two doses in April and June. No more feeds should be given after July, so that the canes have plenty of time to harden up for the winter. The usual multi-nutrient feeds are normally sufficient for the purpose.

Leaf fall

Despite being evergreen, bamboos are continually losing some leaves. Even evergreen plants don't keep their leaves for ever, and each leaf is replaced after a few years. But the leaves are never lost all at once, so there are always plenty of leaves on a plant.

Don't remove the fallen leaves, because they are an important source of nutrients. As they rot, they release silicon, which becomes available to the plant and helps replenish its needs.

Pruning measures

Thinning out bamboo canes

Some of the upright-growing species and varieties are characterised by particularly attractive stems (canes), the effect of which can be much enhanced by careful thinning. The result will be to turn an untidy thicket into an elegant arrangement of canes that draws the eye inwards.

A bamboo cane begins to look unsightly after between five and seven years, so it's a good idea to cut out the oldest canes down to ground level every two or three years. You could remove anything from 10 to 20 percent of the canes according to taste.

Cutting back bamboo mats

Low-growing species and varieties of *Pleioblastus* can easily be trained to form broad carpets of vegetation that can be kept short with hedge trimmers. With time they will spread to form extensive matted carpets that can be cut about twice a year to a desired height of between 5 cm and 30 cm (2–12 in). Larger areas may be cut with a nylon-line trimmer or even a lawnmower that has been adjusted to a high setting.

Winter hardiness

Most bamboos come originally from tropical or subtropical regions of the world, and all the bamboos that we grow in the open air are from eastern Asia. It is therefore not surprising

Some low-growing bamboos can be planted over large areas beneath trees and shrubs. If they are damaged during the winter, they can be cut back to ground level in spring.

that some species are only considered moderately hardy (though *Fargesia* species are extremely hardy).

It's also worth bearing in mind that hardiness depends on a number of different factors apart from the actual temperature. A plant's hardiness is also affected by its position, the local climate, the degree of exposure to wind and even the fertilisation regime. It is therefore difficult to give exact indications as to the hardiness of a particular bamboo.

Winter protection

It is generally possible to avoid frost damage to bamboos by providing suitable winter protection. Such measures are particularly advisable during the first winter after a bamboo has been planted.

The area occupied by the rhizomes can be protected from frost with a layer of dried leaves or straw, which must be removed by the end of March at the very latest. Well-rotted animal manure is also very suitable, besides which it will provide extra nutrients for summer growth.

The best winter protection for bamboos is a good layer of snow, as this protects both the ground and the leaves from the ravages of frost. Don't be tempted to remove snow from the canes, even if they are bowed down under the weight of it. They are extremely elastic and will soon bounce up again afterwards.

To make sure that bamboos are not frozen when there is no snow on the ground, you can protect sensitive species with a layer of mulch made up of leaves and straw. The ground underneath this will only be frozen at the surface, which means the plants will still have access to water.

Watering to prevent winter damage

The most important preventative measure is to give your bamboo plants plenty of water before winter starts. As with most evergreen plants, it is lack of water that damages them in winter. This problem usually occurs towards the end of winter when strong sunlight causes loss of moisture and consequent damage. If the groundwater is frozen, the plant is unable to replenish its supplies, and as a result the leaves dry up and turn brown.

You can help prevent this happening by making sure the

The later in the season bamboos are planted, the more necessary it will be to provide winter protection.

plants start the winter with plenty of water, so that they can survive periods of frosty weather without sustaining too much damage. Check the soil around the plants in November, and if it's dry, give it a thorough soaking. If necessary, you can water the soil again during mild spells in winter.

Repairing winter damage

Even if the leaves are dead, you should always wait before removing the stem. Often the leaves are the only parts to be damaged and new growth will appear in May. However, if no new leaves appear, then the stem must be removed right down to ground level. The bamboo will then put out new shoots.

Propagating bamboos

The best and simplest method of propagation is by division. You can remove sections of a plant and replant them immediately in a suitably prepared location elsewhere.

It is also possible to remove rhizomes provided they have put down roots, though it will admittedly be some time before a new clump of bamboos is fully formed.

Ferns are particularly fond of the shade of trees, where attractive foliage displays can be created in combination with shade-loving perennials.

Planting and maintaining ferns

Ferns are a standard perennial plant, and there is a wide choice of them available at most garden centres. However, if you're looking for a particular species or variety, you may need to look for a specialist nursery of mail-order supplier to fulfil your requirements.

Ferns, like other perennials, are cultivated in the pots in which they are offered for sale. This means they can be planted out at any stage during the growing season. But a particularly favourable time is in the spring, just as the new fronds are developing.

Location requirements

The first prerequisite for growing ferns is finding a position that fulfils their growing needs and keeping it that way.

With the exception of a few rock-loving types, ferns are essentially woodland plants. Woodlands are their natural habitat, providing shelter from strong sunlight and desiccating winds. Woodlands are also characterised by generally damp soils and constant humidity, while the ambient temperature is lower than in the surrounding areas. Most wild ferns grow in the rich humus layer to be found below trees, where they only form superficial roots.

Where to plant ferns in gardens

Location is vitally important if you want your ferns to establish themselves over a long period. Their natural habitat should provide the best indication as to where they should thrive best in your garden.

The most suitable locations are shady or half-shaded areas beneath trees or bushes with deep roots, or alternatively areas next to garden walls or in the shade of the house.

Those ferns that grow among rocks and scree in the wild should be planted in equivalently stony positions. The best locations in a garden might include shady rock gardens or cracks in walls.

Preparing the soil

It is equally important to prepare the soil properly before planting ferns. Ferns grow mainly in humus but form shallow roots. So ideally the soil should be open and rich in humus, with a nicely porous subsoil. If your soil doesn't already fulfil these criteria, then suitable preparation will be required.

You will first need to dig the soil over well to create an open structure. To raise the humus levels, add plenty of leaf compost, peat or a mixture of the two, working this nicely into the topsoil. The heavier the soil, the more of these materials will be needed to create a sufficiently open structure. You will also need to work some 50 g/m² (1.5 oz/sq yd) of hoof and horn into the topsoil to provide a base fertiliser. Finally, add a 5-cm (2-in) layer of humus on top.

Planting

With clump-forming ferns, make sure you don't plant them too shallow, as the rootstock grows gradually upwards. They should be positioned a little deeper in the soil than in the pot in which they arrived.

There is one important exception to this: all the ferns with creeping rootstocks such as *Adiantum* (maidenhair ferns) and *Polypodium* (polypody) should be planted in a shallow position.

After you've finished planting, press the soil down firmly and water thoroughly. Finally, cover the soil with a mulch layer of leaf compost.

Ferns on rocks or walls

Even rock-growing ferns need plenty of space for their roots in the cracks between rocks and stones. You should fill the spaces you have chosen with humus-rich planting compost. Once you have watered the soil and it is firmly established, then the ferns can be planted in it.

Some ferns such as maidenhair spleenwort (Asplenium trichomanes) are particularly suitable for planting in cracks in walls or between rocks.

Maintenance tasks

Being woodland plants, ferns are adapted to the annual leaf fall from deciduous trees and shrubs. The leaves provide natural winter protection and add to the humus in the topsoil.

This means from a gardening point of view that **the autumn leaves must always be left** around ferns. Fern plantings in the shade of walls need to receive a plentiful dose of leaf compost every autumn to make up for the lack of leaves falling on the bed.

It is also important to leave the dead fronds on the plants throughout the winter, as they similarly provide natural protection against the cold. You should hold off from removing the old fronds, whether of deciduous or evergreen ferns, until early spring, just as the new fronds begin to develop. Moreover, with many ferns there is no need to cut out the old fronds at all, as the new ones will simply grow over the top of them.

Providing nutrients

Provided the leaf fall and the old fronds are left throughout the winter, these should provide enough nutrients so that regular feeding is not required.

If, however, this proves insufficient for the ferns' needs every year, then it is sensible to provide a supplementary feed. Some 30–40 g/m² (approximately 1 oz/sq yd) of a multi-nutrient fertiliser should be enough to restore the nutrient balance. Suitable organic fertilisers might include hoof and horn or blood, fish and bone meal.

Raising moisture and humidity levels

Ferns need a constantly damp soil and constant humidity. During dry periods the humidity levels can be enhanced by using a hose with a fine spray device. Humid air is in fact more vital to the plants than damp soil, and regular spraying during hot, dry weather will stop the fronds turning brown prematurely during the high summer.

Frost damage

The best way to avoid frost damage to evergreen ferns is to choose a suitably shady and sheltered position when planting them in the first place. This is because frost damage to ferns occurs mainly as a result of exposure to the wind or to winter sun.

You should always leave the old fern fronds on the plants over the winter, as they provide natural winter protection.

The first stage of spore propagation is the formation of tiny green gameto-phytes, from which the ferns develop.

Propagating ferns

Generative propagation of ferns (i.e. from spores) is a specialist procedure that requires a lot of know-how. Vegetative propagation by means of division is simple and easy to achieve.

Propagating by division

The best time to divide ferns is in spring as the new fronds start to unfurl. First the fern plant is dug up very carefully and any loose soil is removed. Ferns with creeping rhizomes should be cut into small sections with a knife. With clump-forming ferns the constituent plants can simply be prised apart. It's vital to keep any consequent root damage to a minimum, to make sure the resulting plantlets will grow well.

The plantlets should then be grown in pots for six months before being planted out in the garden.

Propagating from spores

Spore propagation is the most productive way of propagating ferns, but it is also the most time-consuming. The best growing medium is pure peat that has been sterilised with boiling water (very little peat is actually required).

The first task is to collect the spores, which ripen at various times between late summer and autumn depending on the species. You can tell the spores are ripe when the sori (clusters of sporangia) change colour from green to brown. The fertile fronds should be cut off and placed in plastic bags. As the fronds start to dry out, so the ripe spores fall out.

They can now be sown immediately. They should be spread thinly and gently pressed into the growing medium. After sowing, the seed trays should be placed in a warm, shaded location and kept moist.

After some four to six weeks they develop into a green carpet of gametophytes or prothalli (the sexual stage of the fern). From these the young plantlets finally emerge. As soon as the first fronds become visible, the plantlets can be pricked out.

at a glance

Grasses
- The best time to plant out is in the spring.
- Deciduous and evergreen grasses should be cut back to ground level in the spring, but not before.
- Clumps that have become bare in the centre should be rejuvenated by division.
- Seedlings from grass varieties should preferably be removed, as they are usually less attractive than the original varieties.
- Sensitive grasses should be covered with a layer of dried leaves in winter.

Bamboos
- Bamboos need plenty of watering during the growing season and before winter sets in.
- They also need plenty of nutrients.
- Fallen leaves should not be removed.
- Winter protection is mainly needed in the year of planting and with more sensitive species.

Ferns
- Fallen leaves should always be left alone as they provide natural winter protection and are an important source of humus and nutrients.
- Old fronds should never be removed until the spring as they also provide winter protection.
- With many species they don't need to be removed at all, as they will soon be covered up by new growth.

Index